ULTIMATE CONDITIONING FOR MARTIAL ARTS

Loren Landow

Human Kinetics

Library of Congress Cataloging-in-Publication Data

Names: Landow, Loren, 1973-
Title: Ultimate conditioning for martial arts / Loren Landow.
Description: Champaign, IL : Human Kinetics, 2016. | Includes bibliographical
  references and index.
Identifiers: LCCN 2015041959
Subjects: LCSH: Martial arts--Training. | Mixed martial arts--Training.
Classification: LCC GV1102.7.T7 L36 2016 | DDC 796.8071--dc23 LC record available at http://lccn.loc.
gov/2015041959

ISBN: 978-1-4925-0615-7 (print)
Copyright © 2016 by Loren Landow

This publication is written and published to provide accurate and authoritative information relevant to the subject matter presented. It is published and sold with the understanding that the author and publisher are not engaged in rendering legal, medical, or other professional services by reason of their authorship or publication of this work. If medical or other expert assistance is required, the services of a competent professional person should be sought.

The web addresses cited in this text were current as of November 2015, unless otherwise noted.

Acquisitions Editor: Tom Heine; **Developmental Editor:** Cynthia McEntire; **Managing Editor:** Nicole Moore; **Copyeditor:** Tom Tiller; **Indexer:** Nan Badgett; **Permissions Manager:** Martha Gullo; **Cover Designer:** Keith Blomberg; **Photograph (cover):** AP Photo/The Canadian Press, Jonathan Hayward; **Photographs (interior):** Neil Bernstein; Adam Bratten for figures 3.29, 4.7, and 6.2; **Photo Production Manager:** Jason Allen; **Art Manager:** Kelly Hendren; **Associate Art Manager:** Alan L. Wilborn; **Printer:** United Graphics

Other credits:

We thank the Muscle Pharm Corporation in Denver, Colorado, for assistance in providing the location for the photo shoot for this book.

Human Kinetics books are available at special discounts for bulk purchase. Special editions or book excerpts can also be created to specification. For details, contact the Special Sales Manager at Human Kinetics.

Printed in the United States of America   10 9 8 7 6 5 4 3 2 1

The paper in this book is certified under a sustainable forestry program.

Human Kinetics
Website: www.HumanKinetics.com

United States: Human Kinetics
P.O. Box 5076
Champaign, IL 61825-5076
800-747-4457
e-mail: info@hkusa.com

Canada: Human Kinetics
475 Devonshire Road Unit 100
Windsor, ON N8Y 2L5
800-465-7301 (in Canada only)
e-mail: info@hkcanada.com

Europe: Human Kinetics
107 Bradford Road
Stanningley
Leeds LS28 6AT, United Kingdom
+44 (0) 113 255 5665
e-mail: hk@hkeurope.com

Australia: Human Kinetics
57A Price Avenue
Lower Mitcham, South Australia 5062
08 8372 0999
e-mail: info@hkaustralia.com

New Zealand: Human Kinetics
P.O. Box 80
Mitcham Shopping Centre, South Australia 5062
0800 222 062
e-mail: info@hknewzealand.com

E6476

ULTIMATE CONDITIONING FOR MARTIAL ARTS

Contents

Foreword

As a college football player, I always knew the importance of a structured strength and conditioning program to maximize my performance. When I shifted my athletic career to mixed martial arts, I knew that having a lengthy history of strength and conditioning along with my skills was going to be an "X" factor in competing with the best in the UFC Heavyweight Division. I worked with Coach Loren Landow while I was preparing for the NFL draft and it was a no brainer to have him as one of my coaches for my MMA career.

It is important for all martial artists to best prepare their bodies for battle. The biggest part of being prepared for competition is having a full and comprehensive plan that accounts for all the training sessions martial artists have during a training week and making sure that overtraining is avoided. Many times, athletes implement strength and conditioning without any direction and assume that because they are doing work or getting tired that it will help them for competition. I have seen athletes sabotage their own performance first hand. Whether it was ridiculous workouts or not understanding that, in many cases, less is more, especially while tapering for competition. Coach Landow always seems to implement speed, agility, strength, power, and conditioning into my program seamlessly, while also always having me in a position that my taper was correct, and I felt amazing going into competition. I think you will find in this book that Loren Landow takes a "leave no stone unturned approach" and his methods always had me ready the night of the fight!

Whether you are a recreational athlete or an elite-level competitor, you can benefit from the structured plan laid out in this book, but you must do the work and be committed to your own success!

Brendan Schaub
UFC Heavyweight and star
of *The Fighter & The Kid* Podcast

Acknowledgments

This book would not have been possible without many key individuals. Brendan Schaub, who was the genesis to my strength coach role for MMA and martial artists, trusted me to prepare him for his career in mixed martial arts and introduced me to many coaches who believed in my abilities; Trevor Whitman, Leister Bowling, Amal Easton, these men allowed me into their training centers and trusted me to be part of their teams, and I will always be indebted to them. To the coaches I have met along the way and shared and learned from; Rener Gracie, Tony Jefferies, Christian Allen, Marc Montoya, Duane Ludwig, Vinnie Lopez, and Eric Telly. All these coaches, we have shared corners in competition and spent time on the road across the world in quest for victory for our athletes, I am truly honored!

Many athletes took a gamble with me preparing them early in my career as a performance coach with martial artists, Brendan Schaub, Shane Carwin, Nate Marquardt, Eliot Marshall, Cody Donavan, Chaun Simms, Jared Hammon, Josh Copeland, Damico Rogers, Todd Duffee, and Justin Wren.

And thank you to the many athletes who continue to trust me in preparation of their careers in martial arts; Neil Magny, Brandon Thatch, Drew Dober, Tony Simms, TJ Dillashaw, Danny Castillo, Cat Zingano, Donald Cerrone, Jarred Mercado, Peter Straub, Bojan Velickovic, Dimitri Veal, Chris Camozzi, Brain Camozzi, Josh Cavan, Bobby Lashley, Dustin Jacoby, Grace Cleveland, Brittany Boone, Brian Foster, Dustin Jacoby, Ian Heinisch, Sid Bice, Marcus Edwards, Jordan Titoni, Randy Rowland, and Brian Rogers.

Thank you to all the models who helped with capturing the exercises in this book: Josh Cavan, Brittany Boone, Grance Cleveland, Eric Bach and special thanks to Whitney Tirrell, who not only served as a model, but put in the time and effort for photo selection and organization of the book, and was more help than she will ever know. And also thank you to Rebecca Simms for assisting with the chapter on recovery and nutrition and Kim Constantainesco for the hours spent on the editing process during this journey!

Thank you to my family. My wife, Michelle, and my beautiful daughters Taylor and Morgan for all the support and the understanding of my time commitment to my craft, I love you all so very much!

Introduction

Welcome to the journey of performance training for martial arts! Whether a person is already a martial artist or has just decided to become one, he or she is hungering for self-betterment. Martial arts teach us that this process is more about the journey than about the destination. With that said, people practice martial arts for various reasons; some people use them as a form of exercise, others as a means of achieving balance in life, and still others for the pleasure of competition. Regardless of the preferred approach to martial arts training, this book can serve as both a resource and a reference. It not only guides martial artists, instructors, and trainers on a path of tactical training, but also serves as accountability as an instructional manual to exercise execution. It presents 120 exercises that range from active dynamic warm-ups to the most explosive exercises for superior results.

This book is the result of my own 18-year search for the optimal training program for sport performance. Along the way, I have made countless errors, questioned common practices, and read literature and research—both good and bad. These years of effort have led me to a simple understanding: Performance training requires a unique blend of science and intuition. We must use science to justify our methods, but, ultimately, experience gives a practitioner the intuition needed for creating the best programs.

The 10,000-hour rule discussed by Malcolm Gladwell in *Outliers: The Story of Success* (2008) plays a role both in strength and conditioning in the martial arts. This rule tells us that in order to master any craft, a person must put in nearly 10,000 hours, or 10 years, of consistent work! For example, as a professional trainer, I have dedicated myself to the craft of preparing athletes to excel in their sport of choice. I have been fortunate enough to work with some of the best athletes in the world, and, regardless of the sport, those who reach the highest levels share one trait—consistency!

Many good training programs have been created, but, at the end of the day, success comes down to the practitioner's consistency. Throughout this book, therefore, you are reminded that training is not about *what* one does but about *how* one does it. This distinction means that intent is the highest priority when considering the transferable qualities of training. For training to be fully functional, it must meet the demands of the chosen sport; furthermore, each practitioner must be assessed individually in order to develop a needs analysis.

With these realities in mind, this book is structured as a series of progressions, much like the belt system used in many martial arts. Each of us must crawl before we walk, walk before we run, and run before we sprint. Whatever role you play in this process—practitioner, instructor, or trainer—I hope you enjoy it! To help you make the most of the journey, this book shows you how to set the right starting point, then provides a training plan to eliminate weaknesses and build on strengths.

The progressions presented in this book are based on levels of competence. As with martial arts belt systems, the content of training is often structured into the categories of beginner, intermediate, and advanced. However, it is entirely possible to be a black belt in a martial arts discipline but a novice in performance training. For this reason, a part–whole teaching technique that divides a certain skill into smaller, more manageable parts is used for all skills presented in the book.

Chapter 1 (Physical Requirements for Martial Arts) identifies the physical attributes that athletes need for martial arts. Athletic ability is made up of several biomotor abilities, including speed, power, strength, agility, flexibility, balance, coordination, and conditioning. The amount of training time to devote to each biomotor ability depends both on the demands of the chosen sport and on the athlete's individual needs.

Chapter 2 (Evaluating Martial Arts Fitness) dives into the process of assessing an athlete's current level of readiness for training. Testing criteria can be based on the biomotor abilities discussed in chapter 1 to sort through a given athlete's personal strengths and weaknesses. The result of this process is commonly known as a needs analysis.

Chapter 3 (Dynamic Warm-Ups and Flexibility) introduces the foundation of the training program. The quality of an athlete's preparation indicates how well she or he will perform. The best preparation for tactical sessions involves active dynamic flexibility, which also helps offset many chronic and overuse injuries incurred by martial artists during training. This chapter includes 41 exercise photos, which show setup and execution.

Chapter 4 (Exercises for Base Conditioning) examines how to condition for a particular discipline depending on its specific demands and on the bodily energy system that takes highest priority in that discipline. More specifically, this chapter explores key energy systems, correlating exercises, and variations of time and intensity to help you identify the necessary training zones for the chosen discipline and the current level of fitness.

Chapter 5 (Exercises for Striking and Kicking) and chapter 6 (Exercises for Wrestling and Grappling) offer a range of strength-building and explosive exercises categorized by purpose (e.g., strikes versus wrestling). Athletes who build a good foundation of muscular endurance can express more strength and therefore more power—the X factor in sport. To help achieve this goal, these chapters present 30 game-changing exercises.

Chapter 7 (Exercises for Speed and Agility) builds on the part–whole teaching method to help athletes fulfill their potential for explosiveness and elusiveness in both training and competition. This chapter presents 20 exercises complete with photos and descriptions of setup and execution.

Chapter 8 (Recovery and Nutrition) covers two key facets of all training. Too often, recovery and nutrition are treated as mere afterthoughts. However, training is a stimulus, and one's ability to adapt well to it depends on implementing daily, weekly, and monthly strategies for recovery and nutrition. This chapter presents nutritional guidance and daily recovery tactics—for both pretraining and posttraining—to help maximize the athlete's time away from the gym.

Chapter 9 (Program Planning and Periodization for Martial Arts) puts all of the training variables together. It can be intimidating to consider the various training options, and in some cases an athlete may not know where to begin. To resolve such confusion, this chapter provides a road map for the competitive year. At its core, periodization is simply a series of timely trade-offs involving the training demands of volume and intensity. The goal is to manipulate those variables in order to elicit the best training response at the optimal time for competition.

Chapter 10 (Programs for the Striking and Kicking Arts) and chapter 11 (Programs for the Wrestling and Grappling Arts) build on the information presented in chapter 9. These chapters take a more art-specific approach to creating programs for individual disciplines, thus giving you the freedom to customize training styles based on the chosen sport.

Chapter 12 (Blending and Customizing Programs for MMA) is, as the title indicates, dedicated to mixed martial arts training. Although MMA is one of the fastest-growing sports in the world, it lags far behind in both instruction and programming for strength and conditioning. The good news is that we can customize a training program for MMA by drawing on the appropriate training methods presented in earlier chapters.

The goal of *Ultimate Conditioning for Martial Arts* is simple: Minimize confusion and maximize individual results. Whether one is brand new to martial arts practice or is a lifelong practitioner, this book is the best resource for fulfilling the passion and drive for self-betterment!

Physical Requirements for Martial Arts

For centuries, martial arts have served as tools for fitness and self-defense. They fulfill these functions—from the adolescent to the elite level—by laying a firm foundation of fundamentals, discipline, and consistency and by providing a long-term systematic process. When martial arts are viewed through the lens of athletic qualities, each discipline is distinguished by its own unique demands; however, many of their athletic needs are similar as shown in figure 1.1.

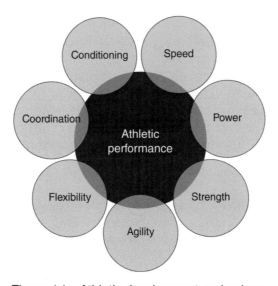

Figure 1.1   Athletic development and subsequent motor abilities.

BIOMOTOR ABILITIES

The building blocks of athleticism are the biomotor abilities: speed, agility, power, strength, flexibility (mobility and stability), balance, coordination, and conditioning. Most athletes can develop the various biomotor abilities concurrently, and this is generally the best approach for both novice and intermediate athletes, who have less training capacity and need to develop multiple abilities simultaneously. Elite athletes, on the other hand, may benefit more from devoting concentrated blocks of training to developing specific abilities. For example, an athlete facing a rigid competition calendar might spend about a month of training (or one mesocycle, as discussed in chapter 9) on speed and power without putting much emphasis on conditioning, which can restrict the full expression of the first two abilities. Because conditioning and speed lie at opposite ends of a continuum, an elite athlete can separate them in training.

Speed

Of all the athletic qualities, speed is the most coveted. From the running speed of a 100-meter sprint to the delivery speed of a kick or punch, speed is a quality that all sport commentators talk about and all athletes exhaust their training to achieve. Speed can also be seen, for example, in a swift judo toss, a blast double-leg takedown, and the mounting of a great defense against a takedown attempt. However you picture it, speed is a quality worth training for.

The muscles that allow an athlete to move fast and produce timely force are governed by the nervous system. As a result, if training is done right, all of the biomotor abilities develop in a complementary fashion. It is crucial, however, to train for speed in an unfatigued state, which can be accomplished through short-distance sprints, resisted sprints, uphill runs, and partner-chase games that create competition (for more information, see the discussion of speed and agility in chapter 7). Be mindful also of the fact that speed depends on technique; never sacrifice technical ability for the sake of short-term performance in a drill.

Agility

Agility separates good athletes from great ones—for example, in the ability to react and explode or to decelerate and transition into a kick, punch, takedown, or redirection of an opponent. This ability can be both an innate gift and a trainable skill. The goal of agility training is to learn how to do the right things from the wrong positions. In combat sports in particular, participants must constantly react and change position based on the opponent's actions. To maximize this ability, athletes can use specific agility drills to develop body awareness that helps them in one-on-one battles and minimizes their risk of injury.

Power

Power is a key component of martial arts success. It adds more snap to kicks and punches and improves one's ability to throw or toss an opponent. As a result, martial arts classes dedicate much time to producing specific power by working on kicks and punches. The power developed in class can be augmented by dedicating separate training time to build general power. There are many ways to do so; for example, sprints, skips, jumps, medicine-ball throws, Olympic-style movements, and other weight-room strategies can help practitioners express more power in the sport of choice. Specific power exercises can be found in chapter 5 (on striking and kicking) and chapter 6 (on wrestling and grappling).

Strength

As stated earlier, the biomotor abilities build on each other. With this in mind, strength may be the most important quality for an athlete to develop because it provides the underpinning for both power and speed. For this reason, the strongest, most powerful athletes are typically also the fastest.

Many qualities of strength are discussed in later chapters; here, the focus is on maximal strength. Maximal strength is the ability to display maximal voluntary contraction against resistance. When discussing strength in numerical values, the three big lifts are the bench press, the squat, and the deadlift. This book, however, presents many ways to express strength. In grappling-based sports—such as wrestling, jujitsu, judo, and Muay Thai (clinch positions)—practitioners need both dynamic and isometric strength in order to finish and defend against takedowns. In mixed martial arts (MMA), fighters need a blend of good leverage and good old-fashioned brute strength in order to exert positional control in the cage and wrist control on the ground.

Flexibility (Mobility and Stability)

In most martial arts, flexibility is critical. It involves not only how bendable a person is but also the strength that he or she possesses in the available range of motion. Meaning that one's flexibility is only as good as one's muscular stability through the entire range of motion. Therefore, mobility and stability are not separate but interrelated qualities.

Influencing mobility and stability is also the reason for using an active dynamic warm-up instead of static stretching. Research has shown that dynamic stretching is superior to static stretching because it reduces the likelihood of injury and enables greater power output (McMillan et al. 2006). If performance is about power and explosion, why use a strategy that inhibits power output in the precompetition phase? Rather, the warm-up should prepare the athlete for the demands of the chosen sport. Therefore, given that competition requires the muscles to shorten and lengthen rapidly under tension, the warm-up must do the same. The active dynamic warm-up presented in chapter 3 is fully detailed and choreographed to provide the best preparation for both practice and competition.

Balance

Balance tends to be overlooked in most training programs. However, like coordination, it requires rehearsal and therefore should be addressed often in training. Balance relies on a blend of the athlete's senses and his or her response to external forces and additional stimuli (whether visual, aural, or tactile). In the martial arts, an athlete's balance in an open-fight stance depends on weight distribution and how well he or she manages the weight on the balls of the feet while in motion. Balance also depends heavily on strength, especially in clinch positions—the stronger the athlete, the better he or she can maintain balance in order to offset an opponent's attempted throw or takedown and transition into a throw or takedown of his or her own.

Coordination

Coordination is the ability to get various body parts working together in a general sense. Many people assume that coordination should be trained only to a limited extent; however, just as strength underpins speed and power, coordination is crucial to speed, power, and agility. For example, the coordination of movements from the ground up helps produce efficient power.

More specifically, good footwork is an essential part of the fundamental coordination required to put oneself in position to strike or defend. Footwork should not be confused with agility, but the two are related. Footwork consists simply of temporal and spatial patterns that help you establish a rhythm, which in turn enables you to move fluidly and produce power. Agility, in contrast, involves movement based on the need to react. The relationship between the two is this: The more coordinated you are and, more specifically, the better your footwork is the more agile you can be. For example, if an opponent throws a kick or punch, good body awareness allows an athlete to counter the strike and move into an offensive position.

Conditioning

In martial arts, performance is governed more by conditioning than by any of the other qualities. In this book, conditioning is divided into two basic types—general and specific—that both need to be developed by athletes at all levels for optimal performance. General conditioning establishes greater work capacity, whereas specific conditioning is tailored to the exact competition demands of a given discipline. Disciplines vary in their approaches to competition, ranging from point sparring to specified rounds and time. Regardless, the goal in conditioning is to develop a great foundation of general fitness that allows the athlete to handle higher intensities of specific work down the road. This specific work mimics the demands put on the body's primary energy systems during competition in the chosen discipline.

The conditioning program presented in this book is built on the following three energy systems (see figure 1.2): alactic (phosphagen), lactic (glycolytic), and aerobic (oxidative). The alactic (phosphagen) system is also known as the ATP-PC system and should be thought of as jet fuel—highly powerful but burns up quickly. It provides the most readily available ATP and is used for brief, explosive bursts. This is a much-needed capacity and one that is trainable if an athlete adheres to appropriate rest intervals that enable him or her to express full power in training. Typically, after 0 to 10 seconds of maximal effort, a person needs about two minutes to restore 80 percent of the fuel used and three minutes to restore 92 percent.

The lactic (glycolytic) system fires up after roughly 20 to 90 seconds of high-intensity work—in that part of the intensity range of training when you feel localized burn, heaviness, and inability to continue repetitions. Most people confuse the burn for lactic acid accumulation, but in fact it results from the accumulation of lactate and hydrogen ions that interfere with muscular contraction. Year-round training of this type is common in many martial arts, and it is extremely popular in MMA training. However, this training should not be done year-round;

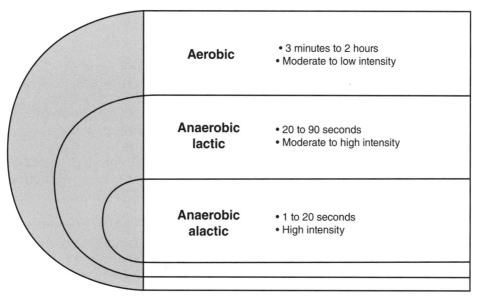

Figure 1.2   Energy system use (time and intensity).

it is extremely taxing on the body and difficult to recover from. Having said that, it is important to implement lactate training no sooner than 4-6 weeks prior to competition to best mimic the intensive nature of the sport. The goal of training this system is to raise the lactate threshold—that is, to push to it but not past it!

The aerobic (oxidative) system is the most important of the energy systems. A good aerobic base sets a foundation for future stages of more intensive training. Furthermore, the broader the base of the aerobic workload, the better the athlete can tolerate more intensive intervals with less detrimental fatigue, thus helping her or him recover sooner from depletion of the more intensive alactic and lactic energy systems (Seiler, Haugen, and Kuffel 2007). Ironically, many martial arts classes use primarily this energy system because the classes last 60 to 90 minutes and involve working at intensity levels that are tough to maintain for that length of time. This combination of duration and intensity makes the aerobic system the top priority for martial arts training.

Many people labor under misconceptions about training, especially about energy systems. In reality, all of the energy systems work simultaneously; the question, then, is which one predominates. The answer depends on two factors—time and intensity of work. For this reason, the goal of *Ultimate Conditioning for Martial Arts* is to help you identify the best plan for the chosen discipline.

DISCIPLINES

There are many martial arts forms to choose from. This book touches on the most popular forms and those that are similar to other art forms.

Karate

Developed in what is now Okinawa, Japan, karate is a highly explosive striking form that involves punches, kicks, knee strikes, elbow strikes, and palm strikes.

Taekwondo

The Korean martial art of taekwondo has been an Olympic event since 2000. It is explosive and typically consists of blocks, kicks, punches, and open-handed strikes; it may also include sweeps and takedowns.

Brazilian Jiu-Jitsu

Brazilian jiu-jitsu is a self-defense system that focuses on grappling and ground fighting. The sport hinges on submissions based on joint locks and chokeholds, but what makes it an amazing art form is the underlying chess match that occurs during rolling to set up the submissions.

Muay Thai

Muay Thai is a combat sport and martial art from Thailand. It is a physical and mental discipline that uses fists, knees, elbows, shins, and feet. Its maneuvers include stand-up striking and various clinching techniques.

Judo

Judo was created in Japan and is now an Olympic sport. Its objective is to throw or otherwise take the opponent to the ground, then either pin the opponent or force a submission by means of a joint lock or choke.

Wrestling

The earliest known wrestling took place in ancient Greece, but many styles have been developed. This Olympic sport is known for grappling, clinch fighting, throws, takedowns, and pins while securing dominating positions.

Mixed Martial Arts

Mixed martial arts (MMA) is a sport that involves all martial arts disciplines. Those used most often are kickboxing, wrestling, jiu-jitsu, and Muay Thai, but many blends of taekwondo and karate are also found in the sport. The primary objective of MMA is to win by submission, knockout, or a judge's decision based on strikes, cage dominance, and positional dominance.

As shown in table 1.1, each martial arts discipline requires a mix of the biomotor abilities discussed earlier in this chapter. With these basics in mind, the following chapters lay out an evaluation and programming process that enables you to forge a plan specific to the needs of both the individual and the sport of choice!

ADAPTATION TO TRAINING

Training results depend on the principle of specific adaptation to imposed demand (SAID); in other words, we get what we train for. The human body adapts to the demands placed on it—as long as we avoid overtraining. Therefore, coaches and athletes need to make smart decisions that complement desired goals. For example, an athlete might use complementary training to prepare for the 100-meter dash by combining short-sprint workouts (to develop speed) and longer sprint distances (to build speed endurance and increase speed reserve). With the proper training and recovery, the short-speed work makes the athlete faster and more explosive. Meanwhile, the speed endurance work enables the athlete to maintain top-end speed longer and carry a more intensive training load.

Table 1.1 Martial Arts Disciplines and Biomotor Abilities

	Karate	Taekwondo	Brazilian jiu-jitsu	Muay Thai	Judo	Wrestling	MMA
Aerobic conditioning	High	High	High	High	High	High	High
Anaerobic conditioning	High	High	Moderate	High	High	High	High
Flexibility	High	High	High	High	Moderate	Moderate	High
Strength	Moderate	Moderate	High	Moderate	High	High	High
Power	High	High	Moderate	High	High	High	High
Speed and agility	High	High	Moderate	Moderate	Moderate	High	High
Balance and coordination	High	High	High	High	High	High	High

In contrast, noncomplementary training might involve running a 5K to become faster in the 100 meters. Of course, this example is ridiculous, but errors of this type are made by many coaches and trainers in all sports. The key point is this: Training must transfer directly to the sport of choice. Otherwise, the athlete is working hard and burning calories—but not getting better at what the chosen sport demands.

Here's another way to think about it. Dynamic correspondence theory states that in order for training to transfer, it must have three qualities: a coordinative relationship, biomechanical relationship, and an energetic similarity. A coordinative relationship means that training includes skills similar to those associated with the chosen sport. The speed of striking and kicking are critical for the martial artist. Learning the skill of relaxation will help him or her utilize the cross-extensor reflex, which is a natural occurring reflex of efficient locomotion of limbs moving in opposition and exactly why great speed coaches teach athletes to relax to maximize this reflex. A biomechanical relationship means that training includes movements using force and velocity in patterns similar to those associated with the chosen sport. Energetic similarity means that the conditioning demands of training are similar to the demands of competition in the chosen sport.

In order to experience adaptation, an athlete must go through a process in which training is the stimulus. In the early phase of training, the athlete may have a performance decrease due to neural fatigue and the process of physiological recovery, as you will see in the Hans Selye model (figure 1.3). From this initial stimulation, training must continue to increase the loads in order to lead to the accumulation phase. After three or four weeks of increased accumulation, it is time for deloading. This weeklong phase lowers the training volume of the

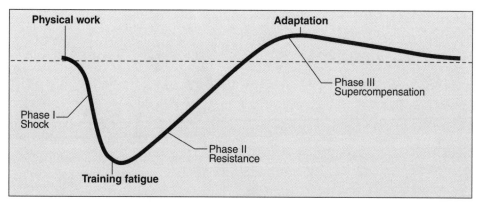

Figure 1.3 General adaptation syndrome theory (response to a stressor).
Adapted from H. Selye, 1956, *The stress of life* (London: Longmans Green).

preceding weeks in order to allow for recovery and let the adaptation process take place so that the athlete reaches a higher level of fitness and performance. To emphasize the point: Gains are made during the deloading or recovery weeks. This is the reason that athletes taper prior to major competitions—to allow the body to catch up to all the work that has been done.

CONCLUSION

Now that you know the general qualities needed by a martial artist, it is time to set an individualized course. This is where the evaluation process begins, and chapter 2 discusses how to use testing to create an individual training plan tailored to the athlete and the chosen discipline. The needs analysis is a blend of subjective and objective evaluation of the athlete's current strength and weakness compared against the demands and needs of the martial art of his or her choice. No matter the outcome of the tests, it is in the best interest of each athlete to train all qualities whether they are a strength or a weakness. The training plan needs to be adaptable based on the training demands of the discipline.

Later in the book (chapter 9), many examples are provided of ways to mix and match training variables in order to create the optimal training plan. However, no course can be set until you determine individual needs through evaluation and understand the best way to apply the various biomotor abilities to the chosen discipline.

Chapter 2

Evaluating Martial Arts Fitness

As world-renowned strength coach Steven Plisk says, "To be a better specialist, one must be a better generalist." For example, to be the best sport performance coach, one must fully understand several subjects, such as anatomy, biomechanics, physiology, biochemistry, programming, and periodization—and be able to use these bodies of knowledge as tools. If instructors and trainers become well versed in the general subjects of athletic ability (biomotor development), programming, and training, they can help athletes get better. In turn, the martial artist can express his or her skill set through more explosive speed, more power in every strike, more strength in clinch positions, and the necessary fitness to compete until the end.

To start training on the right footing, it is necessary to observe the athlete's current fitness level through the lens of performance ability, then create a needs analysis. All athletes possess both strengths and weaknesses, and the evaluation process reveals athletic shortcomings and flags potential injury patterns. The evaluation process covers both the quantitative and the qualitative aspects of biomotor abilities: speed, agility, power, strength, flexibility, and conditioning (table 2.1). The best approach is to obtain baseline numbers before the training program begins, then retest at certain times during the training program and compare those results with the baseline numbers in order to evaluate progress. For many sports (e.g., football, baseball, tennis), a complete database of testing results is available, but that is not yet the case for the diversity of martial arts.

Table 2.1 Performance Qualities, Tests, and Equipment

Performance quality	Test	Equipment
Power	Vertical jump: vertical jump with countermovement, vertical jump without countermovement, vertical jump with chalk Broad jump: broad jump with countermovement, broad jump without countermovement	Vertec device, chalk, tape measure or jump mat as pictured
Power and acceleration (short speed)	10- and 20-yard (or meter) sprints	Cones, stopwatch
Agility	Pro shuttle: agility, balance, and acceleration Long shuttle: agility, short speed, and balance Spider drill: agility, balance, coordination, and flexibility	Cones, stopwatch, tennis balls, tape measure, basket
Speed endurance (long speed)	300-yard (or -meter) shuttle	Cones, stopwatch
Aerobic fitness Max aerobic speed	Cooper test	400-meter track, stopwatch
Upper-body strength and strength endurance	Push-up test	Tennis ball
Core stability	Plank test	None
Shoulder mobility	Apley scratch test	Tape measure or ruler
Hip, knee, and ankle mobility	Squat test	None
Knee stability	Single-leg hop test	None

To obtain accurate numbers and ensure the athlete's safety, it is advisable to spread the tests over multiple days. Otherwise, fatigue can inhibit baseline scores and put the athlete at risk for injury during a maximal testing session. Therefore, before the training program begins, set aside two days for testing that are separated by 48 hours. In addition, to obtain realistic numbers, follow the sequence in this chapter: power tests first and fitness and conditioning tests at the end.

POWER

As stated in chapter 1, power is essential for performance in martial arts. The power tests presented in this section help individualize a training program.

VERTICAL JUMP

There are many ways to test an athlete's vertical jump. Depending on the equipment used, the testing can be either costly or as inexpensive as sidewalk chalk. The method preferred by many strength and conditioning coaches, performance coaches, and personal trainers is a Vertec device or a jump mat (as pictured here). Regardless of the method used, the testing must be done when the athlete is warmed up but not fatigued.

If using a Vertec device, do the following before performing the drill itself: Stand as tall as possible beneath the device. Extend one arm to a maximal vertical reach and mark in inches (or centimeters if you use metric) the standing reach value based on the slats of the Vertec. The colors of the slats signify a specific measurement. All white slats are one-half inch, all blue are one inch, and all red are six inches.

Two vertical jumps using a jump mat are included here—one with a countermovement and one without. Performing the two different jumps enables you to determine more specifically the type of training that the athlete may need. For example, an athlete who displays a higher vertical jump with a countermovement than with no countermovement may possess more explosive ability than sheer strength. In this case, the athlete may be best served by prioritizing work that develops strength. In contrast, if the athlete displays a higher vertical jump with no countermovement, he or she may be best served by prioritizing explosive movements, such as medicine-ball throws and plyometrics (jumps), while still working on strength.

Vertical Jump With Countermovement

Equipment

Jump mat or Vertec device

Procedure

Determine your beginning maximal reach as previously described. Start with your feet separated at a jumping width (about hip-width apart as in figure 2.1a). Move into a squat (figure 2.1b), then quickly reverse direction and push through the ground to jump as high as possible (figure 2.1c). Fully extend one arm to reach as high as possible and land (figure 2.1d). Perform three trials, resting 20 seconds between attempts. Record the average height of the three jumps, then subtract the beginning maximal reach value to determine the vertical jump value.

Figure 2.1 Vertical jump with countermovement: (a) Start position; (b) squat.

Figure 2.1 Vertical jump with countermovement: (*c*) jump; (*d*) land.

Vertical Jump Without Countermovement

Equipment

Jump mat or Vertec device

Procedure

Set the beginning maximal vertical reach (as determined by the standing reach described earlier). Next, assume a squat position with your feet hip-width apart (figure 2.2a). Hold the squat for two seconds, then explode upward while pushing through the ground. Extend one arm and reach as high as possible (figure 2.2b). Repeat for three trials, then record the average height of the three jumps. Subtract the beginning maximal reach value to determine the vertical jump value.

Figure 2.2   Vertical jump without countermovement: (a) squat; (b) jump and extend the arms.

Vertical Jump With Chalk

Not everyone has access to a Vertec device or jump mat. If you don't, there are other practical ways to measure vertical jump height. As with the jump mat version, the test can be done either with a countermovement (as described here) or without a countermovement.

Equipment

Chalk, wall, tape measure

Procedure

Hold a piece of sidewalk chalk in one hand and stand perpendicular to a wall. Stand tall and extend one arm overhead as high as possible. Mark the wall with the chalk at the highest point you can reach (figure 2.3a). This mark indicates your beginning maximal reach. Reset into a ready position. Swiftly drop into a squat (figure 2.3b) and explode upward for maximal height. At the apex of the jump, tap the chalk against the wall to record your highest jump (figure 2.3c). Use a tape measure to measure the distance between your reach height and your jump height. Perform three trials and record your average value.

Figure 2.3 Vertical jump with chalk: (a) establishing beginning maximal reach; (b) dropping into a squat; (c) marking the highest point of the jump.

BROAD JUMP

The broad jump is easy to measure and helps determine the athlete's power. All that is needed is a tape measure.

Again, two types of broad jump are presented, one with a countermovement and one without. If the athlete jumps farther with the countermovement than without it, this is a good indication that she or he should prioritize strength work while still working on explosive exercises to complement power output. If, on the other hand, the athlete performs better without the countermovement, he or she may want to prioritize explosive exercises while still implementing strength work to complement power output.

Broad Jump With Countermovement

Equipment

Tape measure

Procedure

Stand at the front of the tape with your feet hip-width apart (figure 2.4a). Drop quickly into a squat position (figure 2.4b) and drive forward with as much force as far as possible (figure 2.4c). Stick the landing and measure from the back heel (figure 2.4d). Perform three trials and average the results.

Figure 2.4　Broad jump with countermovement: (*a*) stand with feet hip-width apart; (*b*) drop into squat position; (*c*) drive forward; (*d*) stick the landing.

Broad Jump Without Countermovement

Equipment

Tape measure

Procedure

Stand at the front of the tape with your feet hip-with apart. Drop into a squat position and hold the squat for two seconds. Explode out of the squat and jump as far as possible. Perform three trials. Average the distance.

POWER AND ACCELERATION (SHORT SPEED)

The power test results of the vertical and broad jump can be further substantiated by the 10- and 20-yard (or meter) sprint, which require energy system usage similar to that of the jumps. All of these tests relate to sport performance because the power of an athlete's sprinting and jumping correlates directly with the power of his or her kicking and striking.

10- and 20-Yard (or Meter) Sprints

Equipment

Cones (three), tape measure, two stopwatches

Procedure

These sprints provide a fantastic way to further test power, as well as the athlete's ability to show explosive acceleration. Measure out the two distances—10 and 20 yards (or meters); mark the start and finish lines with cones and position a timer at each finish line. The runner starts in a two-point stance with the lead foot on the start line. Each timer starts the stopwatch on the runner's first movement and stops the stopwatch when the runner crosses the finish line at the specified distance. Perform three trials at each distance, then average the times for each distance.

AGILITY

Agility is a key requirement for a martial artist. The more agile the martial artist is, the better he or she can attack or maneuver around an opponent's attack.

AGILITY, BALANCE, AND ACCELERATION

The pro shuttle is a unique drill that simultaneously tests the athlete's agility and balance. When a martial artist can control the body while moving laterally, and while decelerating at each line touch, he or she gains a sense of true body control.

Pro Shuttle

Equipment

Three cones, tape measure, stopwatch

Procedure

Place three cones in a straight line, spaced 5 yards (or meters) apart for a total distance of 10 yards or meters (figure 2.5). Face the middle cone as though straddling a line with a hand down in a three-point stance. Run 5 yards (meters) to the right and touch the line where the cone is with your right hand. Immediately change direction and sprint 10 yards (meters) to the left to the far cone. Touch the line where the cone is with your left hand. Quickly accelerate to the right and run past the starting line (middle cone). The timer starts the stopwatch on your initial movement and stops the stopwatch when you run through the last line. Repeat the drill but this time start to the left. Average the two times.

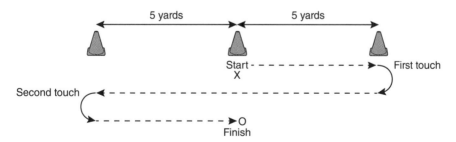

Figure 2.5   Pro shuttle.

AGILITY, SHORT SPEED, AND BALANCE

The long shuttle further tests the athlete's long speed (speed endurance) while also challenging agility and balance in the starting and stopping at each line. To get even more sense of body control, assess the athlete's weight distributions at each line touch.

Long Shuttle

Long shuttle is a unique drill that tests an athlete's straight-line speed and ability to change direction.

Equipment

Four cones, tape measure, stopwatch

Procedure

In a straight line, place four cones 5 yards (meters) apart—that is, at intervals of 0, 5, 10, and 15 yards (meters). Begin at the first cone in a three-point stance (figure 2.6). Accelerate as quickly as possible to the cone positioned at the 5-yard (-meter) mark, touch the line with your right hand, rapidly change direction, and return to the start line. Touch the start line with your right hand, then accelerate to the cone positioned at 10 yards (meters). Touch the line with your right hand and quickly return to the start line. Touch the start line with your right hand, then accelerate to the cone at 15 yards (meters). Touch the line with the right hand and sprint back through the start line. The timer starts the watch on your first movement and stops the watch as you pass the start line for the final time. Rest for 90 seconds, then repeat the drill. Average the times of the two trials.

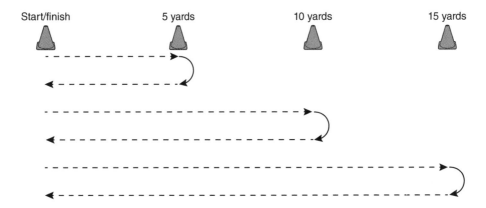

Figure 2.6   Long shuttle.

AGILITY, BALANCE, COORDINATION, AND FLEXIBILITY

The spider drill provides a great way to showcase athleticism in action: acceleration, change of direction, balance, coordination, and flexibility. It also creates a highly competitive environment when multiple athletes perform the drill together.

Spider Drill

Equipment

Five tennis balls, basket

Procedure

Set up for the drill by placing five tennis balls in a rectangle shape and one tennis ball at the midpoint from the far side of the rectangle (figure 2.7). All tennis balls should be about seven yards from each other and the two on the same side as the basket should be seven yards from the basket left and right, which is the midpoint of the near long line of the rectangle. Place a basket at the starting point. Stand in an athletic position at the starting point. Run to a tennis ball, pick it up, and return the ball to the basket at the start position. You can retrieve the balls in any order, but you must always use the same hand to pick up the ball. Pick up all five balls, one at a time. Follow a 1:3 work-to-rest ratio and repeat the drill using the opposite hand to pick up the tennis balls. Compare the two trials and note differences in coordination, flexibility, and agility on the two sides.

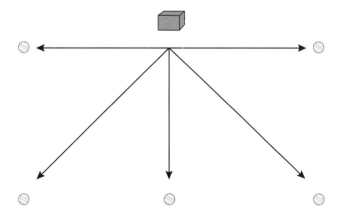

Figure 2.7   Spider drill.

SPEED ENDURANCE (LONG SPEED)

Speed is the X factor in sport; however, success also depends on the ability to *repeat* high-intensity efforts, especially in the late portions of a match or round. One great way to give the martial artist a sense of his or her ability to repeat high-intensity efforts is to use the 300-yard (or -meter) shuttle.

300-Yard (or -Meter) Shuttle

This shuttle is a grueling test that reveals an athlete's ability to produce speed under fatigue, which is essential to sport.

Equipment

Two cones, tape measure, stopwatch

Procedure

Place the cones 50 yards (or meters) apart on a flat surface. Begin on the start line at one of the cones and run to the far cone. Touch the cone with your right hand, run back to the starting cone for a total distance of 100 yards (meters), and touch the cone with your left hand. Repeat twice more for a total of 300 yards. The timer starts the stopwatch on your initial movement and stops the stopwatch when you cross the finish line. Rest for three times as long as it took you to complete the test; for example, if the test took you one minute, rest for three minutes. Next, repeat the test a second time. The goal is to produce similar numbers from first trial to second.

AEROBIC FITNESS

Aerobic or base fitness is a must for all disciplines. Developing a broad aerobic base enables the martial artist to tolerate a higher workload of intensive effort.

Cooper Test

Equipment

Track, stopwatch

Procedure

The Cooper test is a good, inexpensive way to test your $\dot{V}O_2$max. Performing the test is as simple as going to the local high school track. Run as many laps as possible for 12 minutes, then use the following equation to estimate your $\dot{V}O_2$max:

$$(35.97 \times \text{miles run}) - 11.29 \text{ or } (22.35 \times \text{kilometers}) - 11.29$$

For example:

$(35.97 \times 1.5 \text{ miles run}) = 53.96 - 11.29 = 42.67$ (estimated $\dot{V}O_2$max) and
$(22.35 \times 1.5 \text{ kilometers run}) = 33.5 - 11.29 = 22.21$ (estimated $\dot{V}O_2$max)

Note your results and retest regularly to track improvement.

UPPER-BODY STRENGTH AND STRENGTH ENDURANCE

The push-up test provides a good way to assess either upper-body strength or strength endurance based on a foundation of fitness. For example, a younger athlete or a person who is new to training will probably perform fewer repetitions than a more experienced athlete because of his or her limited foundation of training; as a result, this person's test result will indicate strength more than strength endurance. In contrast, for athletes with more training experience, the push-up test may serve as more of a strength endurance test based on the number of repetitions they complete.

Push-Up Test

Equipment

Tennis ball

Procedure

Depending on one's ability, the test can be performed either in a traditional push-up position or in a modified knee position. Place the tennis ball on the ground at the level of the sternum. With your hands at shoulder width and your elbows out slightly from your sides, slowly and deliberately lower your sternum to the ball (figure 2.8a). Once contact is made, push back up to the start position (figure 2.8b). Do as many repetitions as possible.

Figure 2.8   Push-up test: (a) lower sternum to tennis ball; (b) push back up to start position.

CORE STABILITY

Power is transferred by means of the trunk or core. The stronger and more stable the midsection is, the more power an athlete can produce. To test this capacity, we can use the plank test.

Plank Test

Equipment

Stopwatch

Procedure

Set up in a forearm plank position, aligned from ear to ankle. Your hips, knees, and ankles should all be in alignment with each other. Your elbows should be under your shoulders, and your forearms should be parallel (figure 2.9). The timer begins the stopwatch once you are in position and stops it when you demonstrate instability three times in any of the following ways:

- Loss of core integrity (drop in the low back)
- Change in posture of the head or hips based on fatigue
- Global muscular fatigue, as noted by tremors or shaking

At this point, the test is done. The maximum time for the plank test is 60 seconds.

Figure 2.9   Plank test.

SHOULDER MOBILITY

Overuse injuries are common in martial arts, especially in the shoulder joint. Fortunately, a martial artist may be able to avoid injury and lost training time by assessing shoulder range early in training.

Apley Scratch Test

The Apley scratch test provides a great way to check shoulder range of motion, both internally and externally, while the arm is either extended or flexed at the glenohumeral joint—the main shoulder joint, located between the shoulder blade and the upper arm bone.

Equipment

None

Procedure

Stand tall. Externally rotate the humerus and flex the shoulder and elbow. The opposite elbow is flexed with the humerus rotated internally and the shoulder extended (figure 2.10). From this position, make a fist with each hand without altering postural position. A coach or trainer measures the distance between the fists. Repeat with the same motions on the opposite sides and again measure the distance between the fists. Note any asymmetries. If any pain is felt, consider having it checked prior to beginning a full training program.

Figure 2.10   Apley scratch test.

HIP, KNEE, AND ANKLE MOBILITY

Avoiding overuse injury in the lower extremities is critical to a martial artist's success. To this end, the squat test helps identify potential range-of-motion asymmetries in the ankles, knees, and hips that could lead to lost training time if not identified early on.

Squat Test

Equipment

None

Procedure

Start in an athletic position (figure 2.11a). Perform five squats, using three seconds on the descent and three seconds on the ascent (figure 2.11b). Note the depth of the squat, the knee position, the foot position, and any pain. (The depth of the squat is determined based on the position of the tops of the thighs in the lowest squat position in relation to the ground: above parallel, at parallel, or below parallel.) If any pain is felt, consider having it checked prior to beginning a full training program.

Figure 2.11 Squat test: (a) start position; (b) squat.

KNEE STABILITY

Lower-body injuries, especially knee injuries, run rampant in all sports; therefore, a high-quality training program needs to identify high-risk and low-risk athletes. The primary knee ligaments that provide stability to the joint include the anterior cruciate ligament (ACL), the medial collateral ligament (MCL), the lateral collateral ligament (LCL), and the posterior cruciate ligament (PCL). The risk of injury to these ligaments increases if joint integrity is not optimal. In addition, the knee ligaments are protected by dynamic support from the muscles of the hips, trunk, thighs, feet, and ankles. If an athlete lacks sufficient strength and stability, the ligaments must handle more load in the end ranges of motion. However, because ligaments are not as elastic as muscles, they may rupture if they are asked to do too much.

Single-Leg Hop Test

Equipment

None

Procedure

This knee stability test consists of five hops on each leg. Jump one repetition at a time and try to stick the landing with minimal collapse of the knee, either in or out (figure 2.12). Perform five hops on your right leg, then five hops on your left leg. If you experience pain or issues in controlling the landing, you may be considered at high risk for injury. High-risk athletes should prioritize single-leg strength and balance exercises; low-risk athletes should practice them as well.

Figure 2.12   Knee stability test: (*a*) single-leg hop; (*b*) sticking the landing.

TESTING AND RETESTING

Repeatability of testing is crucial for legitimizing the results. Therefore, warm-ups, test sequencing, and environment should be consistent across tests in order to standardize the results of the pretest and all subsequent tests. Retesting determines whether training is truly helping the athlete achieve the desired goals. To allow for the best possible numbers, all retests should be completed after an active recovery week or a deloading week of training. The ideal is to test two or three times per year to help monitor all performance qualities as they can change over the training year.

After you have collected testing results, it is easier to determine an effective starting point for training—that is, the start of optimal preparation for optimal performance. Due to the lack of sufficient data specific to various martial artists, it is most important to compare a given athlete's baseline numbers to the results of retests to determine the improvement produced by training.

CONCLUSION

The next step in the process is to lay the foundation for effective training. To that end, the warm-up, covered in the next chapter, prepares the athlete for training and provides corrective exercises for the overuse and overcompensation that martial artists typically incur during training. The warm-up is performed systematically to allow for optimal preparation prior to both training and competition.

Chapter 3

Dynamic Warm-Ups and Flexibility

Once you have completed the initial testing and prepared an individual needs analysis, it is time to get on the road to performance training for martial arts. The way in which a martial artist prepares indicates how he or she will perform, and this chapter enables you to set the foundation for effective athletic preparation.

Many warm-ups consist of arbitrary exercises, such as jogging laps, performing static stretches, jumping rope, or executing a series of butt kicks and high-knees. All of these are good forms of exercise, and each serves a purpose, but a warm-up must be more systematic and progressive in order to increase the athlete's range of motion through higher contractile velocity—just like the demands of a sport. The active dynamic warm-up presented here consists of a series of exercises, each of which in itself constitutes a skill that must be developed and refined over time.

Furthermore, we must change our perspective on the warm-up process and go beyond the traditional rationale. For many warm-ups, the rationale hinges on increasing the heart rate, inducing perspiration, and increasing core body temperature; these effects, however, are merely by-products of good old-fashioned exercise, and performance training has evolved over the past 20 years. We now know that a sound, structured, active, dynamic warm-up can help an athlete develop the very biomotor abilities that make up athletic performance—speed, agility, power, strength, flexibility, balance, coordination, and conditioning. This perspective enables us to see that the warm-up provides a chance to lay a broad foundation of skills; indeed, it may be the best tool in the athlete's training toolbox.

FOUR STAGES OF SKILL ACQUISITION

Motor skill acquisition doesn't come overnight. Whether learning a new submission technique, a new defensive strategy, or a front kick for the first time, one must work through a four-stage process to mastery. The four stages are unconscious incompetence, conscious incompetence, conscious competence, and unconscious competence. Some stages last longer than others, but all build on each other; therefore, a martial artist must be consistent in his or her training approach.

In the first stage—unconscious incompetence—the new skill is introduced. At this point, the athlete is either consumed with not knowing how to do the skill or afraid of looking foolish in front of peers. He or she applies the skill poorly or perhaps does not even attempt it. In the second stage—conscious incompetence—the athlete is no longer consumed by apprehension but still cannot perform the skill. He or she does, however, understand how to complete the skill. In the third stage—conscious competence—the athlete can reproduce the skill, but only with conscious effort. In the final stage—unconscious competence—the skill has become automatic; that is, the athlete can perform it with no conscious effort.

This four-stage model of motor-skill development explains why teaching is imperative for performance training. The earlier an athlete understands the how and why of an exercise, the less time it takes her or him to master the exercise. At that point, the exercise progression can become more seamless and fluid.

THREE-STAGE PROGRESSIVE WARM-UP

The warm-up is an extremely valuable tool. Indeed, the true value of a consistent, active, dynamic warm-up will be apparent before competition. For many athletes, nerves run high before competition, but athletes are creatures of habit, and starting the competition preparation with a warm-up that has become a ritual helps put the athlete in a state of effective focus and progressive arousal.

The warm-up sequence presented here follows a three-stage progression: muscle activation, dynamic flexibility, and transit mobility. Each exercise description includes a list of the main muscles focused on by that exercise.

Muscle Activation

The preparation series begins with muscle activation exercises, including the quadruped series, the straight-leg series, the hip rotation series, the squat series, and the shoulder series. These exercises provide low-intensity activation of the hips and core in order to lay a foundation of mobility and stability prior to more intensive warm-up exercises. All of the series in the muscle activation category should be done with intent and focus.

QUADRUPED SERIES

For all exercises in this series, perform five repetitions. Begin in a kneeling position with six points of contact with the ground: two hands, two knees, and the toes of both feet. The hands are directly under the shoulders, the knees are under the hips, and the toes are pulled toward the shins (figure 3.1). This setup is used for all of the quadruped exercises.

Figure 3.1 Beginning position for all exercises in the quadruped series.

Fire Hydrant

Muscle Focus

Tensor fasciae latae, gluteus medius (anterior fibers)

Equipment

None

Procedure

Push the hands firmly into the ground with the core braced. Move one thigh out to the side in abduction (figure 3.2). At the end of the range, hold for a two-second count, then return the thigh to the start position. Complete five repetitions. The range of motion is limited to what you can control without moving other joints, such as the elbows, spine, or hips. Switch legs and perform five repetitions with the new leg.

Figure 3.2 Fire hydrant.

Hip Circle

Muscle Focus

Tensor fasciae latae, gluteus medius (anterior and posterior)

Equipment

None

Procedure

Push the hands firmly into the ground with the core braced. Move one knee in a circular motion (figure 3.3), either counterclockwise or clockwise. Complete five repetitions, then switch legs. Make sure that no additional movement comes from the spine or upper body.

Figure 3.3 Hip circle.

Scorpion

Muscle Focus

Rectus femoris, gluteus maximus

Equipment

None

Procedure

Push the hands firmly into the ground. Slightly draw one knee toward the head into hip flexion (figure 3.4a). Move the thigh back into hip extension while maintaining a 90-degree angle at the knee (figure 3.4b). Simultaneously, pull the toes of the moving leg toward the shin (dorsiflexed position). Hold for a two-second count without moving any other joints. Complete five repetitions, then switch legs.

Figure 3.4 Scorpion: (a) hip flexion; (b) hip extension.

Lateral Leg Reach

Muscle Focus

Quadriceps, tensor fasciae latae, gluteus medius (anterior), internal and external obliques

Equipment

None

Procedure

Push the hands firmly into the ground. Fully extend one leg straight back with the toes pulled toward the shin (figure 3.5a). Externally rotate the thigh and abduct the leg as far as possible (figure 3.5b) without movement in other joints. Hold for a two-second count, then return the leg to the start position. Complete five repetitions, then switch legs.

Figure 3.5 Lateral leg reach: (a) leg straight back; (b) leg abducted as far as possible.

Cat/Cow

Muscle Focus

Erector spinae, quadratus lumborum, latissimus dorsi, trapezius, thoracolumbar fasciae

Equipment

None

Procedure

Push the hands firmly into the ground. Slowly arch the spine as high as possible while tucking the hips (figure 3.6*a*). Slowly lower the spine into an extended position while tilting the hips (figure 3.6*b*). Complete five repetitions.

Figure 3.6   Cat/cow: (*a*) arch spine into cat; (*b*) lower spine into cow.

Bird Dog

Muscle Focus

Gluteus maximus, erector spinae, deltoids, latissimus dorsi, trapezius

Equipment

None

Procedure

Begin in the quadruped position. Brace the core and with minimal movement of the spine (figure 3.7*a*), extend the opposite arm and leg into extension (figure 3.7*b*). Maintain a braced core position to avoid a lateral drop in the pelvis and minimize too much lumbar extension and switch sides (figure 3.7*c*).

Figure 3.7   Bird dog series: (*a*) brace core; (*b*) extend opposite arm and leg; (*c*) switch sides.

STRAIGHT-LEG SERIES

For all exercises in this series, perform five repetitions with each leg. All of the exercises are performed while lying on the ground. Lie in a fully extended position with the ears, shoulders, hips, knees, and ankles aligned. The body orientation varies between prone, supine, and side lying, but the posture remains constant.

Supine High Kick

Muscle Focus

Rectus femoris, sartorius, iliopsoas

Equipment

None

Procedure

Assume a supine position with one knee bent and the opposite leg straight (figure 3.8a). Brace the core, tighten the thigh of the straight leg, and lift that leg as high as possible without bending the knee or altering the hip position (figure 3.8b). Hold for a two-second count, then repeat. Perform five repetitions, then switch legs.

Figure 3.8 Supine high kick: (a) start position; (b) lifting the leg.

Side-Lying Abduction

Muscle Focus

Gluteus medius, quadratus lumborum

Equipment

None

Procedure

Lie on one side in proper alignment (figure 3.9a). Brace the core, tighten the thigh of the upper leg, pull the toe toward the shin, and abduct the thigh 30 degrees (figure 3.9b). Hold for a two-second count, then repeat. Perform five repetitions, then switch legs.

Figure 3.9   Side-lying abduction: (a) start position; (b) abducting the thigh.

Side-Lying Adduction

Muscle Focus

Adductor magnus, gracilis, adductor longus, pectineus, adductor brevis

Equipment

None

Procedure

Lie on one side in proper alignment. Brace the core and move the top leg into a hip-flexed position (figure 3.10a). Tighten the thigh of the bottom leg, pull the toe toward the shin, and lift the leg off the ground just a couple of inches while maintaining extension of the bottom leg (figure 3.10b). Hold for a two-second count, then repeat. Perform five repetitions, then switch legs.

Figure 3.10   Side-lying adduction: (a) start position; (b) lifting bottom leg.

Prone Abduction

Muscle Focus

Gluteus maximus, adductor magnus, gluteus medius (posterior)

Equipment

None

Procedure

Lie in a prone position in proper alignment. Brace the core and extend the right arm out to the side as in one side of the letter T (figure 3.11*a*). Tighten the thigh and gluteus maximus of the left leg while pulling the toes toward the shin and lifting the leg two inches (about five centimeters) off the floor. Slightly abduct the thigh to 20 degrees (figure 3.11*b*) and hold for a two-second count. Perform five repetitions, then switch legs.

Figure 3.11   Prone abduction: (*a*) start position; (*b*) lifting the left leg.

HIP ROTATION SERIES

The hip rotation series provides a great way to further account for the potential joint ranges of motion of the hip before training or competition.

Supine Hip Rotation

Muscle Focus

Piriformis, obturator internus and externus, quadratus femoris, gemellus superior and inferior

Equipment

None

Procedure

Lie flat on the ground with the knees flexed and the feet in the toes-up position (figure 3.12a). Anchor the heels into the ground and slowly pivot the opposite knee to the opposite heel (figure 3.12b). The pivot points of the movement should be the heels. Alternate sides and complete eight repetitions per side.

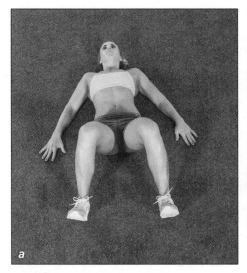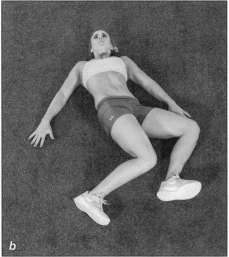

Figure 3.12 Supine hip rotation: (a) start position; (b) knee pivot to opposite heel.

Seated Hip Rotation

Muscle Focus

Piriformis, obturator internus and externus, quadratus femoris, gemellus superior and inferior

Equipment

None

Procedure

Sit on the ground with the knees flexed and the feet in the toes-up position (figure 3.13a). Anchor the heels to the ground and slowly pivot the opposite knee to the opposite heel (figure 3.13b). The pivot points of the movement should be the heels. Flex the torso over the lead thigh and reach the opposite arm to maximize the stretch on the upper extremity, then alternate sides and complete eight repetitions per side (figure 3.13c).

Figure 3.13 Seated hip rotation: (a) start position; (b) knee pivot to opposite heel; (c) flex the torso while reaching opposite arm.

Supine Hip Bridge

Muscle Focus

Gluteus maximus, erector spinae

Equipment

None

Procedure

Lie flat on the ground with the knees flexed and the feet in the toes-up position (figure 3.14*a*). Anchor the heels into the ground and slowly push straight through the heels to extend the hips while bracing the core (figure 3.14*b*). Slowly return the hips to the ground and repeat. Complete eight repetitions.

Figure 3.14 Supine hip bridge: (*a*) start position; (*b*) hip extension.

SQUAT SERIES

This fourth series in the warm-up focuses on mobility of the ankle, knee, and hip joints. Complete all repetitions with the intent of maximizing the range of motion while maintaining good mechanics. Perform eight repetitions of all exercises at a slow, deliberate pace.

Ankle Rockers

Muscle Focus

Gastrocnemius, tibialis (posterior and anterior), peroneus longus, extensor digitorum longus, extensor hallucis longus, peroneus tertius

Equipment

None

Procedure

Stand with the feet hip-width apart. Rock the body weight forward up to the toes as high as possible (figure 3.15a). Once at the apex of the toe position, lower and shift the weight to the heels while pulling the toes up toward the shins (figure 3.15b). Complete eight repetitions.

Figure 3.15 Ankle rockers: (a) up on the toes; (b) back on the heels.

Body-Weight Squat

Muscle Focus

Quadriceps, hamstrings, gluteus maximus, erector spinae

Equipment

None

Procedure

Stand with the feet hip-width apart or slightly wider; if needed, point the toes out slightly (figure 3.16a). Set the hips back and slowly lower into the squat position (figure 3.16b). Ensure that the knees are in line with the toes and that the heels remain flat on the ground. Complete eight repetitions.

Figure 3.16 Body-weight squat: (a) start position; (b) squat.

Toe Grab

Muscle Focus

Hamstrings, gluteus maximus, erector spinae, soleus, gastrocnemius

Equipment

None

Procedure

Stand with the feet hip-width apart or slightly wider. Grab the toes and slowly lower the hips toward the heels (figure 3.17a). This part of the exercise is fantastic for working on ankle range of motion. Reverse direction and move the hips up while extending the knees (figure 3.17b). This part of the exercise provides a great stretch for the hamstrings. Ensure that the knees are in line with the toes and that the heels remain flat on the ground. Complete eight repetitions.

Figure 3.17 Toe grab: (a) lower hips toward heels; (b) lift hips and extend knees.

Trunk Rotation

Muscle Focus

Internal and external obliques

Equipment

None

Procedure

Stand with the feet hip-width apart. Extend the arms straight out to the sides in a T position (figure 3.18a). While maintaining a flat-footed stance, rotate to one side as far as possible while looking straight forward (figure 3.18b). Alternate sides and complete eight repetitions per side.

Figure 3.18 Trunk rotation: (a) start position; (b) rotation.

Flexed Trunk Rotation

Muscle Focus

Internal and external obliques, rectus abdominis

Equipment

None

Procedure

Stand with the feet hip-width apart and the arms extended in a T position. Bend at the waist while maintaining a flat back (figure 3.19*a*). Rotate to one side as far as possible while keeping the feet flat and looking at the ground (figure 3.19*b*). Alternate sides and complete eight repetitions per side.

Figure 3.19   Flexed trunk rotation: (*a*) start position; (*b*) rotation.

SHOULDER SERIES

Not unlike the quadruped series, this series increases range of motion while providing stability to the joint at the end of the range. The series should be performed slowly and deliberately with great intent and focus. Perform eight repetitions of each exercise.

Bent-Over Scapular Retraction

Muscle Focus

Serratus anterior, rhomboid major and minor, middle trapezius

Equipment

None, dumbbell (optional)

Procedure

Stand with the feet hip-width apart. Bend at the waist so that the torso is parallel to the ground. Fully extend the arms with the fingers toward the ground. Set the shoulders down and back, then pinch the shoulder blades toward the spine while keeping the shoulders down (figure 3.20a). Hold for two counts. Flair the shoulder blades far away from the spine (3.20b), then repeat (3.20c). Complete eight repetitions.

Figure 3.20   Bent-over scapular retraction: (a) pinch shoulder blades toward spine; (b) flair shoulder blades away from spine; (c) repeat.

Bent-Over T

Muscle Focus

Serratus anterior, rhomboid major and minor, middle trapezius, posterior deltoid

Equipment

None, small weight (optional)

Procedure

Stand with the feet hip-width apart. Bend at the waist so that the torso is parallel to the ground. Fully extend the arms with the fingers toward the ground (figure 3.21a). Set the shoulders down and back, then pinch the shoulder blades toward the spine while keeping the shoulders down. Raise the arms laterally to the T position and hold for a two-second count (figure 3.21b). Return the arms to the sides and flair the shoulder blades away from the spine. Complete eight repetitions.

Figure 3.21　Bent-over T: (a) extend arms; (b) pinch shoulder blades toward spine.

Bent-Over 90/90

Muscle Focus

Serratus anterior, rhomboid major and minor, posterior deltoid, infraspinatus

Equipment

None, weight plates (optional)

Procedure

Stand with the feet hip-width apart. Bend over at the waist so that the torso is parallel to the ground. Fully extend the arms with the fingers toward the ground. Set the shoulders down and back, then pinch the shoulder blades toward the spine while keeping the shoulders down (figure 3.22a). Row the elbows to the plane of the back with the elbow and shoulder joints at 90-degree angles (figure 3.22b). Next, externally rotate the arms as far as possible and hold for a two-second count (figure 3.22c). Internally rotate the arms to the row position and extend the arms fully to the start position. Flair the shoulder blades away from the spine, then repeat. Complete eight repetitions.

Figure 3.22 Bent-over 90/90: (a) bend over so torso is parallel to the ground and pinch the shoulder blades toward the spine; (b) row elbows to the plane of the back;(c) flair the shoulder blades away from the spine.

Dynamic Flexibility

As the warm-up progresses, so does the kinetic-chain demand, meaning that a more complete approach of warm-up exercises from head to toe will be implemented. The same parameters of postural alignment apply, just as mentioned in the muscle activation portion of the warm up, and should be treated as a top priority. Remember that joint position dictates muscle function; therefore, if posture isn't maintained, the muscular system works at a disadvantage and is more susceptible to repetitive stress injury. The exercises included in this series develop the biomotor abilities of balance, coordination, flexibility, and strength.

Knee Hug

Muscle Focus

Gluteus maximus, erector spinae

Equipment

None

Procedure

Stand tall in good alignment from the ears through the shoulders, hips, knees, and ankles (figure 3.23a). Lift one leg toward the chest while maintaining a fully extended down leg with that foot flat (figure 3.23b). Drive the down foot through the ground while tightening the gluteus maximus. Alternate legs and complete five repetitions on each leg.

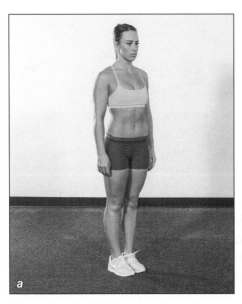

Figure 3.23 Knee hug: (a) start position; (b) knee lift toward chest.

Quadriceps Stretch

Muscle Focus

Quadriceps, rectus femoris, sartorius, iliopsoas

Equipment

None

Procedure

Stand tall in good alignment from the ears through the shoulders, hips, knees, and ankles. Grab one foot with the opposite hand and pull the thigh back past the hip while pulling the heel toward the gluteus maximus (figure 3.24). Maintain extension in the down leg and drive that foot through the ground while tightening the gluteus maximus. Complete five repetitions with each leg.

Figure 3.24   Quadriceps stretch.

Leg Cradle

Muscle Focus

Piriformis, gluteus maximus, quadratus femoris, gemellus superior and inferior, obturator internus and externus

Equipment

None

Procedure

Stand tall in good alignment from the ears through the shoulders, hips, knees, and ankles. Pull one leg up and rotate it externally 45 degrees (figure 3.25). While pulling the knee toward the nose, drive the down heel through the ground and tighten the gluteus maximus. Alternate legs and complete five repetitions on each leg.

Figure 3.25   Leg cradle.

Flexed Hip and Knee Adduction

Muscle Focus

Internal and external obliques, adductor longus, adductor brevis, pectineus

Equipment

None

Procedure

Stand tall in good alignment from the ears through the shoulders, hips, knees, and ankles. Lift one leg to 90 degrees of hip flexion. Use the opposite hand to push into the knee of the lifted leg (figure 3.26). Stabilize through the core and the down leg to avoid rotating the torso. Alternate legs and complete five repetitions per leg.

Figure 3.26   Flexed hip and knee adduction.

Flexed Hip and Knee Abduction

Muscle Focus

Tensor fasciae latae, gluteus medius (anterior)

Equipment

None

Procedure

Stand tall in good alignment from the ears through the shoulders, hips, knees, and ankles. Lift one leg to 90 degrees of hip flexion. Use the hand on the same side to push into the outside of the knee of the lifted leg (figure 3.27). Stabilize through the core and the down leg to avoid rotating the torso. Alternate legs and complete five repetitions on each leg.

Figure 3.27   Flexed hip and knee abduction.

Straight-Leg March

Muscle Focus

Hamstrings, gastrocnemius, gluteus maximus

Equipment

None

Procedure

Stand tall in good alignment from the ears through the shoulders, hips, knees, and ankles. Kick one leg forward while reaching the opposite hand toward the toes (figure 3.28). Keep the down leg straight and the torso tall to maximize the stretch in the hamstrings. Alternate legs and complete five repetitions on each leg.

Figure 3.28   Straight-leg march.

Toe Touch

Muscle Focus

Hamstrings, gastrocnemius, erector spinae

Equipment

None

Procedure

Stand in a staggered position with the lead leg straight and the back leg slightly bent (figure 3.29a). Hinge at the waist while maintaining a flat back. Reach down toward the lead foot to stretch the hamstrings (figure 3.29b). Once at full stretch, extend the hips and reach the arms to the sky (figure 3.29c). Alternate legs and complete five repetitions on each leg.

Figure 3.29 Toe touch: (a) start in a staggered position; (b) reach down toward foot; (c) at full stretch, extend hips and reach to the sky.

Inchworm

Muscle Focus

Hamstrings, gastrocnemius, erector spinae, gluteus maximus, tibialis (posterior)

Equipment

None

Procedure

Start in a push-up position in good alignment from the ears through the shoulders, hips, knees, and ankles. Push the hands firmly into the ground with the arms fully extended (figure 3.30a). Slowly walk the feet forward toward the hands, anchoring each step with the ball of the foot (figure 3.30b). Walk as far as possible without bending the knees. Walk far enough to feel a comfortable stretch on the hamstrings (figure 3.30c-d). Walk the hands forward to get back to the push-up position or into hip extension if not painful. Perform five repetitions.

Figure 3.30   Inchworm: (a) push hands firmly into ground; (b-d) walk the feet forward toward the hands far enough to gently stretch the hamstrings.

Elbow to Instep

Muscle Focus

Rectus femoris, sartorius, iliopsoas, adductor longus, adductor brevis, pectineus

Equipment

None

Procedure

Stand tall in good alignment from the ears through the shoulders, hips, knees, and ankles (figure 3.31*a*). Step into an exaggerated lunge position and place the hand opposite the front leg on the ground. Bring the elbow on the same side as the front leg to the ankle of the front leg (figure 3.31*b*). Keep the torso, shoulders, hips, and head square in the direction of the lunge. Push with the front leg and stand tall with the feet together. Alternate legs and complete five repetitions per leg (figure 3.31*c*).

Figure 3.31 Elbow to instep: (*a*) start position; (*b*) one hand on ground; other elbow to instep; (*c*) alternate legs.

Walking Scale

Muscle Focus

Hamstrings, gastrocnemius, tibialis (posterior), adductor magnus, gluteus maximus

Equipment

None

Procedure

Stand tall in good alignment from the ears through the shoulders, hips, knees, and ankles (figure 3.32a). Step forward with one leg, keeping a slight bend in the knee. Slowly bend at the waist while the torso and the unloaded leg move to a position in which they are parallel to the ground (figure 3.32b). Keep the core braced and maintain good balance and focus. Return to the standing position. Alternate legs and perform five repetitions per leg.

Figure 3.32   Walking scale: (a) start position; (b) torso and leg in parallel position.

Transit Mobility

The last portion of the warm-up addresses transit mobility. These exercises develop not only balance, coordination, and flexibility, but also power, strength, agility, and speed. Remember, the warm-up is structured in progressive stages to achieve optimal timing so that the martial artist is best prepared to showcase his or her skill set, whether in practice or in competition. For that reason, the exercises included in this portion of the warm-up are more explosive and are performed much faster than those in previous stages. In addition, these exercises work all muscles in the body.

Tall Side Slide

Muscle Focus

Total body

Equipment

None

Procedure

Stand tall with the weight on the balls of the feet. Perform jumping jacks (figure 3.33) with the legs and arms while moving laterally. Push off of the balls of the feet to drive the body laterally while simultaneously swinging the arms from hip position to overhead. Increase momentum and distance with each jumping jack. Continue for 20 yards (or meters) down and another 20 back for a total of 40. Rest for 20 seconds, then repeat the exercise by going in the other direction.

Figure 3.33   Jumping jack position in the tall side slide.

Low Side Slide

Muscle Focus

Total body

Equipment

None

Procedure

Start in slight squat position with the weight on the balls of the feet. Perform jumping jacks with the legs and the arms, moving laterally while staying low by keeping the legs in a slight squat position (figure 3.34). Push off of the balls of the feet to drive the body laterally while simultaneously swinging the arms from hip position to the overhead position. Increase momentum and distance with each jumping jack. Continue for 20 yards (or meters) down and another 20 back for a total of 40. Rest for 20 seconds, then repeat the exercise by going in the other direction.

Figure 3.34   Jumping jack position in the low side slide.

Carioca

Muscle Focus

Total body

Equipment

None

Procedure

Start in an athletic position with the weight on the balls of the feet. Rotate the torso and hips while moving laterally (figure 3.35): right foot in front of left foot, left foot out to side, left foot in front of right foot, right foot out to side. Continue for 20 yards (or meters) down, then 20 back for a total of 40 yards. Rest for 20 seconds and repeat by moving in the other direction.

Figure 3.35 Carioca: (a) start position; (b) right foot in front of left foot; (c) left foot in front of right foot.

Carioca Knee Punch

Muscle Focus

Total body

Equipment

None

Procedure

Repeat the carioca pattern but punch the trailing leg to a high-knee position while rotating the torso and hips (figure 3.36). Continue for 20 yards (or meters) down and 20 back for a total of 40 yards. Rest for 20 seconds and repeat by moving in the other direction.

Figure 3.36   Carioca knee punch.

Linear Skip

Muscle Focus

Total body

Equipment

None

Procedure

Stand tall. Walk into a skipping action (figure 3.37). Drive the arms and legs for 30 yards (or meters). Rest for 20 seconds, then repeat in the opposite direction to bring the total ground covered to 60 yards (meters).

Figure 3.37   Linear skip.

Straight-Leg Skip

Muscle Focus

Total body

Equipment

None

Procedure

Stand in good alignment from the ears through the shoulders, hips, knees, and ankles (figure 3.38a). Kick and double-bounce on the down leg (as in a small jump-rope hop). Aggressively drive the kicking leg straight in front of the hips (figure 3.38b) while alternating legs. Keep the posture tall and the core braced to maximally drive through the hips. Continue for 20 yards (or meters).

Figure 3.38 Straight-leg skip: (a) start position; (b) drive leg in front of hips.

Side Shuffle

Muscle Focus

Total body

Equipment

None

Procedure

Start in a slight squat position with the weight on the balls of the feet. Push laterally on the trailing leg (the right leg if you are moving to the left) and quickly get the foot back to the ground (figure 3.39). Drive for 20 yards (or meters) down and 20 back for a total distance of 40 yards. Rest for 20 seconds and repeat by moving in the other direction.

Figure 3.39   Side shuffle: (a) push off of trailing leg; (b) return foot to ground.

In and Out

Muscle Focus

Total body

Equipment

None

Procedure

Start in an athletic position with the weight on the balls of the feet. Rapidly move the feet in (figure 3.40a) and out (figure 3.40b) with as much speed as possible while maintaining the athletic position. Repeat for two sets of six seconds each with 20 seconds of recovery between sets.

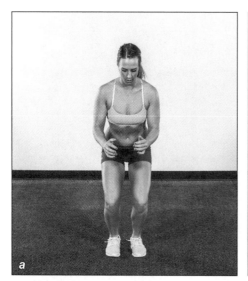 

Figure 3.40   In and out: (a) feet in; (b) feet out.

Lateral A Skip

Muscle Focus

Total body

Equipment

None

Procedure

Stand tall in good alignment from the ears through the shoulders, hips, knees, and ankles with the weight on the balls of the feet. While skipping laterally, punch one knee vertically while driving the opposite leg down to the ground with a double bounce (figure 3.41). Continue for 5 yards (or meters) down and 5 back for a total of 10. Rest for 20 seconds and repeat while facing the other direction.

Figure 3.41   Lateral A skip.

Backward A Skip

Muscle Focus

Total body

Equipment

None

Procedure

Stand tall in good alignment from the ears through the shoulders, hips, knees, and ankles with the weight on the balls of the feet. While skipping backward, punch one knee up and drive the opposite leg to the ground (figure 3.42). Skip for 10 yards (or meters).

Figure 3.42   Backward A skip.

CREATING A WARM-UP ROUTINE

With some 40 exercises to choose from, this menu provides a linear warm-up progression that can also be rearranged to suit the athlete's preferences and any limitations (e.g., time and availability of open space). Once the athlete has learned the skills and rehearsed the warm-up, it should take 12 to 15 minutes.

As the athlete gets used to the process, certain growing pains may occur. An athlete who has gone through the full active dynamic warm-up may notice asymmetries in range of motion between the left and right limbs during the muscle activation and dynamic flexibility exercises. An athlete may also have difficulty holding core stability and maintaining body alignment. Over time, these asymmetries tend to become more balanced, and holding alignment becomes a mere afterthought.

The transit-mobility series requires great coordination and balance. With this challenge in mind, make sure to establish a smooth, rhythmic tempo before increasing the speed of the movements. Remember, athletic movements should be relaxed yet controlled; speed comes as athletic competence rises.

An athlete who does not invest the needed time in a full warm-up must understand that his or her potential for injury is therefore much greater. In addition, the more consistently a martial artist uses a good warm-up, the sooner he or she notices a transfer of the athletic biomotor abilities through the warm-up alone. The transit mobility exercises especially help lay the skill foundation for the later qualities of speed and agility while also providing good general conditioning.

In addition to warming up, one of the best ways to offset injury and begin recovery is to purposefully cool down. A cool-down not only decreases core body temperature and heart rate but also reestablishes a good range of motion after a taxing practice. Effective ways to cool down include the muscle activation and dynamic flexibility exercises. If doing an active dynamic warm-up every day seems redundant, remember that the only way to get better at the skill acquisition involved in these exercises is to do them daily with a specific sequence and intent.

CONCLUSION

Now that the body is prepared, we can ask it to work. Chapter 4 (Exercises for Base Conditioning) lays a foundation involving all of the body's energy systems and establishes a best-practice approach for the martial art of your choice. The better conditioned an athlete is, the better he or she can display primary biomotor abilities and skill. A martial artist who is in better condition can express more speed, power, and strength in the chosen discipline. Again, we need to look in depth at the demands of each martial arts discipline. For example, the timing and number of matches in competition play a role in deciding how to best design a conditioning plan for a given martial artist.

Chapter 4

Exercises for Base Conditioning

In all martial arts, ability depends heavily on skill development, but it is equally important for the athlete to develop good base conditioning. If two martial artists possess similar skill sets, the person with the broader or more established aerobic and anaerobic systems holds the upper hand. The martial artist who can throw punches and kicks with more power in the later portion of a round or a competition enjoys a massive advantage. Building a great foundation of conditioning also helps the athlete maintain coordination longer, thus allowing for more high-quality work in training sessions.

Despite these distinct advantages, discussions of conditioning are often marked by misunderstanding. The confusion results in large part from misinterpretations of current research that tend to sell a trend instead of a science-based practice. In some cases, it is also driven by complete fabrications about how athletes train in order to sell products or systems.

In contrast, the goal of this chapter is to enable you to keep training simple and effective. Three great ways to start taking responsibility for base conditioning are to determine maximum target heart rate (220 minus age), use a 10-point scale to measure rating of perceived exertion (RPE), and track resting heart rate on three mornings per week. Determining the maximum target heart rate allows the martial artist to accurately quantify his or her training intensity for the session based on percentage of the maximum target heart for the given workout. For example, if a twenty-year-old athlete has a low intensity workout in a 60-65% zone of maximum target heart rate, the heart rate range for that training session should be 120-130 beats per minute. Tracking the resting heart rate gives the athlete the tools to chart his or her progress; specifically, as the athlete's base conditioning improves, his or her resting heart rate values steadily decline. Once the conditioning and training become more intensive, the resting heart rate can also be used as an inexpensive tool for helping avoid overtraining syndrome. Charting the trend of resting heart rates over the course of training is a good indication if the conditioning program is helping. Checking it three or four mornings per week, the athlete should notice a steady decline in the resting heart rate values as conditioning becomes better. Now, if the athlete starts to notice an undulating pattern of low to high, this can be a red flag for the athlete to catch a potential overtraining syndrome and make the necessary changes to the training to get the body back on the right course. Decreasing workloads, increasing caloric intake, increasing sleep, and adding more recovery sessions and or days are just a few ways to recalibrate the training process to return the athlete to the right path.

The rating of perceived exertion (RPE) is a subjective gauge of exercise intensity versus an objective measure only. During the training program, a subjective awareness can help the athlete best determine if they are becoming more fit or overtraining or simply having a bad day by tracking RPE values through the course of training.

As stated earlier in chapter 1, Hans Selye's model of general adaptation syndrome theory illuminates the essence of training—and of overtraining. As training stress accumulates, it produces one of two effects: overtraining or adaptation. If the training was correct and the rest was strategically timed, the training should lead to adaptation. However, if the target was missed, overtraining could result. Potential indicators of overtraining include chronic fatigue, decreased appetite, decreased physical and emotional drive, increase in common colds and other infections, chronic muscle and joint pain, and an elevated resting heart rate. One way to prevent overtraining is to consistently track resting heart rate, which, if elevated above the athlete's baseline, can be a red flag for overtraining syndrome.

THREE ENERGY SYSTEMS

In this chapter, the body's use of energy is viewed as falling into three categories: anaerobic alactic, anaerobic lactic, and aerobic. These categories can be further divided into subcategories, but these three suffice for our purposes here. All of the energy systems work at the same time, but the primary responsibility shifts between them depending on the duration and intensity of activity. The real beauty of these energy systems lies in the fact that they complement each other to produce fuel for the body (figure 4.1). As a result, a more developed aerobic system leads to a more efficient anaerobic system; likewise, the metabolic by-products created in the anaerobic system can be used as fuel for the aerobic system.

This interrelatedness is also involved in a common problem in martial arts training. Even though training both aerobic and anaerobic systems concurrently provides more complete preparation, martial artists typically train only one or the other. More specifically, many conditioning-based circuits or intervals used by martial artists require more work by the anaerobic system than by the aerobic system. For optimal results, however, training should match the demands of the sport—without excluding any of the energy systems.

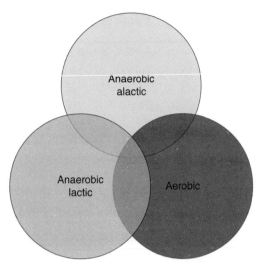

Figure 4.1   The three energy systems.

The *anaerobic alactic system* produces the fuel needed for short, explosive bursts of high-power output—usually up to 12 to 20 seconds—that allow the athlete to really use his or her fast-twitch capabilities. Examples include an explosive throw in judo or wrestling, an explosive strike of the fist, and a spinning back kick.

The *anaerobic lactic system* produces the fuel needed for high-intensive efforts lasting 20 to 90 seconds. During this intensity and duration of activity, the body produces the metabolic by-products lactate and hydrogen, which may contribute to fatigue. This effect typically coincides with the feeling of muscular failure and the deep burn of an exercise. Examples include clinch positions in takedown attempts and defenses, submission setups and attempts, and the maintenance of the top position on opponent, where long periods of "tug of war" and highly fatiguing isometric contractions happen.

The *aerobic system* produces the fuel needed for exercise of long duration (several minutes to several hours) and of low to moderate intensity. This system should be established first, because it provides a broad foundation on which to build the other systems. Whether the discipline is more endurance based (e.g., jujitsu) or more explosive (e.g., taekwondo), all athletes need to work on both aerobic and anaerobic qualities to maximize their conditioning. Having said that, building the base of aerobic fitness is a priority for the martial artist. The foundation it provides allows the artist to best express greater power later in competition. It is also the best way to maintain good coordination for effectively using a chosen skill set.

AEROBIC TRAINING

For most martial arts, the most commonly used way to build an aerobic base is to perform typical roadwork, or outside running. This is a common practice among wrestlers, strikers, and many other martial artists. This type of training can be done in various ways, but the main parameters to manipulate are duration and heart rate zone. A good starting point is to run two or three times per week for at least 12 to20 minutes with the heart rate of 130 to 150 beats per minute to set a broad foundation for most martial arts. As the athlete's fitness improves, aerobic sessions can be lengthened to 60 to 90 minutes. This activity does not necessarily need to be interval based; one can use a flat load of continuous work.

Although the duration of the sessions will increase, it is not advisable to increase the number of sessions per week. The reason is that too much pure aerobic work can compromise the time to develop strength, power, and speed. Remember that the goal here is to use all training to produce the desired end result of optimal sport performance. Since speed and power tend to be the X factors in sport, conditioning must complement, not hinder, the athlete's ability in these areas.

However, increasing the aerobic base can help raise the lactate threshold—the point at which an activity transitions from aerobic to anaerobic lactic, thus causing an accumulation of lactate and the simultaneous release of hydrogen ions. As this accumulation increases, the rate at which a muscle can contract slows down, and fatigue sets in on the working tissue. Aerobic capacity conditioning can be done with any cyclical activity—for example, swimming, running, rowing, and cycling.

As a martial artist builds a better fitness foundation, training can be expanded to include acyclical actions, such as shadow boxing, light rolls in jiu-jitsu, and drilling in wrestling practice. Acyclical actions are more random and help the athlete develop more functional and coordinative patterns of activity. Therefore, as a martial artist increases his or her fitness base, acyclic training offers a great way to emphasize conditioning while working on technique.

For the martial artists I work with, as they increase the frequency of their tactical sessions, I count those sessions as base fitness work and pull out any additional roadwork or cyclical activity until the next off-season program. This adjustment helps avoid overtraining and constitutes the best-practice approach since it helps the conditioning program complement the martial art—a win-win scenario. Too often in martial arts training, tactical sessions are so long that the athlete cannot maintain high intensity; as a result, the sessions mimic base aerobic conditioning in terms of duration and heart rate. The problem is that too much low-intensity work can severely diminish both power and speed. This loss, of course, is a large problem in mixed martial arts and in many other disciplines that use more of an old-school philosophy.

There are also other ways to work on aerobic capacity, even in the weight room. For example, one nice variation on traditional aerobic work involves doing four exercises consecutively (commonly known as circuit training) on minimal rest while maintaining high repetitions (12 to 20 slow and deliberate repetitions). If, on the other hand, an athlete seeks low-impact aerobic work, endurance work can be complemented with swimming. Not only is swimming a good way to work the entire body, but also, due to its low-impact nature, it can serve as an active recovery session.

The aerobic system can be prepared with either of two mind-sets: a focus on aerobic capacity (12 to 90 minutes) or a focus on aerobic power (3 to 12 minutes). Developing aerobic capacity lays the foundation that allows the aerobic system to become broader. To this end, performing work of lower intensity and longer duration allows the athlete to maintain a higher level of more intensive work later in training. Aerobic power, in contrast, requires work of short duration but high intensity relative to the demands of the aerobic system; for example, one could implement a five minute interval with the heart rate range 145 to 150, and use active recovery for two minutes at a lower heart range 120 to 125 and repeat for a total of three reps. Each set is done for five minutes with two minutes of active recovery.

After considering all of these variables, use the methods that best suit individual needs. Make sure to vary the approach sufficiently to avoid stagnation, but always design the sessions in a way that complements the rest of the training program.

AEROBIC CAPACITY

Aerobic capacity training requires 12 to 90 minutes of continuous low-intensity effort with the heart rate in the range of 120 to 150 beats per minute. This work can be as simple as taking a brisk walk, swimming, or doing exercises with traditional cardiovascular gym equipment (e.g., elliptical machine, stationary bike, treadmill, stair climber). All of these modes of exercise can be done with consistent resistance and heart rate; then, as the athlete gains fitness, he or she can be challenged with more of an interval style of aerobic capacity and power blended workout.

For example, to challenge my athletes, I like to pick the mode of exercise that best suits an individual for a 30-minute interval referred to as a 5-4-3-2-1. This work involves a simple but effective use of undulated workload intensity. A treadmill is used in the following description (figure 4.2).

Heart rate can be measured by a heart rate monitor, a heart rate sensor like those found on most cardio equipment, or fingertip palpation of the distal radius for a pulse. Count the number of beats in 10 seconds, then multiply by six.

Treadmill 5-4-3-2-1 Intervals

Equipment

Treadmill

Procedure

Figure 4.2   Treadmill 5-4-3-2-1 interval.

Begin with a five-minute warm-up on the treadmill at a brisk walking pace of 3.6 to 4 miles (5.8 to 6.4 km) per hour (see table 4.1). After five minutes, increase the speed to a jog or light run that can be tolerated with relative comfort. After five more minutes, return the treadmill to the walking speed for four minutes. Next, increase to a running speed at a tempo that can be controlled but is more challenging. After four minutes of running, drop the speed to the walking pace for three minutes, then speed up the treadmill even faster for a three-minute run. This run should be done at a fairly challenging tempo in order to produce a good spike in heart rate.

Table 4.1   Treadmill 5-4-3-2-1 Intervals

	Minutes	Pace
Warm-up	5	Brisk walk: 3.6 to 4 mph (5.8 to 6.4 km)
Jog or light run	5	Well-tolerated jogging speed
Walk	4	Brisk walk: 3.6 to 4 mph (5.8 to 6.4 km)
Run	4	Controlled but challenging run
Walk	3	Brisk walk: 3.6 to 4 mph (5.8 to 6.4 km)
Run	3	Challenging tempo
Walk	2	Brisk walk: 3.6 to 4 mph (5.8 to 6.4 km)
Run	2	Higher than challenging running pace
Walk	1	Brisk walk: 3.6 to 4 mph (5.8 to 6.4 km)
Run	1	Fastest running speed
Cool-down	5	Moderate walk

After this three-minute run, bring the speed back down to the walking speed for two minutes. Next, raise the treadmill to a higher speed that can be sustained for two minutes of running. Return again to the walking speed, this time for one minute, then finish off with one last run at the fastest speed you can maintain for one minute. Finally, return the treadmill to a moderate walk for five minutes to allow for a full cool-down. Note that, with each minute of the cool-down, the heart rate drops. As the aerobic base improves, you will notice the heart rate drops faster into the recovery range of 110 to 130 beats per minute.

ANAEROBIC LACTIC TRAINING

The anaerobic lactic system becomes a priority when the demand for energy increases quickly. This system provides the fuel for high-intensity efforts of 20 to 90 seconds. At the upper end of this range, lactate is produced, a deep burn is felt in the muscles, and muscular failure occurs. At this point, the energy systems create a complementary outcome thanks to the fact that lactate can be converted to pyruvate and then used for aerobic metabolism. In a nutshell, the anaerobic lactic system provides fuel more rapidly, but the aerobic system can sustain the production of fuel for a longer time. Therefore, in planning athletic preparation, these two systems should be thought of not as exclusive but as complementary.

The anaerobic pathway can be divided into lactic capacity and lactic power. When developing lactic capacity, the goal is to push the heart rate at a slightly lower level than that of the lactic threshold but also sustain the working effort for the upper end of the energy system's capacity (typically 90 to 150-180 seconds of high effort). This exact level depends on the athlete's current fitness; for example, an untrained athlete may have a capacity of only 20 to 30 seconds of effort in a given exercise.

In any case, the goal is to put the body into a state in which it can adapt to the increase in blood lactate, ultimately buffering the end ranges of accumulation better and prolonging raising the lactate threshold. This effect can be achieved in many ways but most commonly is done through circuit work. For example, a circuit of three or four exercises that last 30 to 45 seconds each allows the athlete to work in the time needed to reach the upper end of lactic capacity. While doing such circuits and high-intensity intervals, one must allow full rest and restore the heart rate to 110 to 130 beats per minute to enable best success in subsequent sets.

ANAEROBIC LACTIC CAPACITY

One of the best ways to build lactic capacity is to pick a mode of exercise that is cyclical—for example, biking, swimming, sprinting, marching with a sled, using a VersaClimber, or doing body-weight exercises (e.g., lunges). The interval of work should be determined by the athlete's current level of fitness and the chosen mode of exercise. Not all exercises are created equal; indeed, some are much more difficult than others, and the athlete must make a best-practice choice based on his or her ability.

In order to train safely and effectively, it is important to monitor the athlete's heart rate and rating of perceived exertion (RPE). RPE measurements are simple and can be used to determine effort; for example, 1 is easy and 10 is maximal. This approach makes the martial artist responsible for either pulling back or pushing forward with effort to match the corresponding training goal. Increasing capacity requires accumulating volume without hitting the anaerobic threshold too quickly. To buffer and raise the lactate threshold, use tiered sets and repetitions to raise lactate accumulation, then follow up with ideal rest to lower it before beginning the next set. This strategy extends the volume of work without exceeding the lactate tolerance.

The weighted sled march described here is a sample exercise only; each individual has a different capacity, and the sets and repetitions can be adapted in whatever sequence the athlete needs based on his or her current fitness. The sled push typically requires a good amount of weight plates on the sled in order to maintain a marching tempo. Therefore, a martial artist with a lower fitness level may find the exercise so taxing that he or she is unable to perform the exercise long enough to activate the proper energy system before accumulating too much fatigue. Such an athlete may be better served by performing a body-weight exercise—for example, step-ups on a box that is 12 to 16 inches high (about 0.3 to 0.4 m).

In addition, an athlete may experience too much wear and tear having multiple training sessions the same day. In this case, swimming provides a great way to work on conditioning while avoiding the stress of pounding the body against the ground. This can be done with the same energy system goals just as long as the interval times match.

Weighted Sled March

Equipment

Sled, weights

Procedure

Add enough weight to the sled so that you can lean into it without moving it. While holding the leaning position, march with a slow, deliberate tempo for 30 seconds (figure 4.3). Rest for 30 seconds, then repeat. Complete four repetitions (or fewer if an RPE level of 6 is exceeded) on a 10-point scale. Rest for 90 to 120 seconds, then begin another set. Again, complete four repetitions (or fewer if an RPE level of 8 is reached). Once this level has been attained, rest for another 90 to 120 seconds before starting the last set. For this last set, the RPE level should hit 9 or 10.

Figure 4.3 Weighted sled march.

ANAEROBIC LACTIC POWER

Anaerobic lactic power can be trained concurrently with lactic capacity. Training lactic power gives the martial artist the ability to produce power under fatigue. The intervals are shorter in duration but higher in intensity, and they include a nearly full recovery of 1:4 or 1:6 work to rest ratio or with the heart rate returning to 110 to 130 beats per minute before the next repetition. Again, many modes (swimming, bike sprints, versa climber) of exercise can be used, but sprints may be the most effective. Again, many modes of activity can be used either cyclically, such as the bike, treadmill, elliptical or swimming, but sprinting may be best option. The athlete can also choose to use acyclical strategies, such as bodyweight circuits or even more sport-specific activities such as pummeling, heavy bag, or mitt sessions with the tactical coaches.

Sprint Intervals

Sprinting provides a great workout, but it is also a skill that must be learned and implemented with good technique. For this reason, chapter 7 (Exercises for Speed and Agility) is a resource to help martial artists learn the progressions of sprinting correctly.

Equipment

Ideally, a flat grass or turf surface or running track

Procedure

Perform a sprint at 80 to 85 percent of full effort for 20 to 40 seconds (figure 4.4), followed by a walk-back recovery. The walk back should take one to three minutes and return the heart rate to 110 to 130 beats per minute. As with anaerobic capacity training, the goal here is to avoid crossing the lactate threshold and to allow for high power output with a higher volume of work. Perform six to eight repetitions. The repetitions can be clustered into two sets of three or four repetitions with a rest of two to three minutes between sets.

Figure 4.4   Sprint interval.

ANAEROBIC ALACTIC TRAINING

The alactic energy system is the human body's primary fuel source for brief effort of very high intensity. Such efforts typically involve a burst of work ranging from a split second to 20 seconds—for example, an explosive kick, a hip toss to the ground, or a rapid combination of punches. The downside of the alactic energy system is that it comes with a cost measured in time. Specifically, it refuels slowly, optimally taking three minutes per explosive effort, though not all exercises are created equal.

The best way to express the explosive nature of this energy system is through high-velocity exercises (e.g., medicine-ball throws, jumps, and sprints) and high-force exercises (e.g., Olympic lifts, such as the clean and jerk, which is covered in chapters 5 and 6). Typically, high-velocity exercises cause less accumulative fatigue and can be used in repeated actions to build greater work capacity in this system. High-force exercises, on the other hand, tend to cause more fatigue both in the alactic system and in the central nervous system. Due to the greater effort demands of the high-force exercises, as well as the complexity of the lifts, full rest should be taken; in other words, high-force exercises should be used not to build alactic capacity, but to build alactic power.

ANAEROBIC ALACTIC CAPACITY

Developing anaerobic alactic capacity requires working just under the maximal ability of the alactic system in order to allow for more repeated bouts. This approach means keeping intensity just slightly lower than maximal to allow the martial artist to increase volume using that specific energy system. Alactic work tends to be done at an RPE level of 9 or 10 (maximal effort). However, the intensity can be decreased to a level that allows the athlete to repeat the drill without degrading the skill level or increasing the risk of injury. As discussed in the following drill, sprint ladders offer a great way to achieve this effect because the athlete uses the walk-back as an active recovery from each of the specified sprints.

Sprint Ladder

Equipment

Cones (four), flat surface (e.g., grass, turf, or running track)

Procedure

On a flat surface, place cones at 0, 10, 20, and 30 yards (or meters) from a starting point (figure 4.5). At a running speed of 85 to 100 percent of full effort, sprint 10 yards to the first cone, then walk back for a rest interval. Next, sprint

Figure 4.5　Sprint ladder.

20 yards (to the second cone) and walk back. Then sprint to the third cone and walk back. Without taking any further rest, repeat the sprints in descending order—to the 30-yard (third) cone, then to the second cone, and finally to the first cone. Walk back for a rest after each sprint. Rest for two to three minutes after completing the full series of six sprints. Repeat for two or three sets, resting between each set.

ANAEROBIC ALACTIC POWER

Olympic lifts offer a fantastic way to increase alactic power; however, performing these lifts correctly, with the most possible transfer to sport performance requires years of dedicated training. If your access to a gym is limited, you can use short sprints, lightly loaded resisted sprints, and plyometrics to help express knockout power.

Partner-Resistance Run

Equipment

Bullet belt or towel

Procedure

Use a resistance belt (figure 4.6), a towel, or a partner's resistance from the hands (figure 4.7). If using a belt, attach it around your waist. Lean aggressively and begin a punch–drive (refer to chapter 7) action of the legs in a running motion for 5 to 10 yards or meters.

Figure 4.6   Bullet-belt resistance run.

Figure 4.7   Partner-resistance run.

Remember, the body doesn't know distance; it knows time. If a drill is done for 5 to 10 yards, you must account for the time it took to do it. In this drill, the duration should be 3 to 10 seconds—no more! This restriction allows the proper fuel to be used. In contrast, performing a resisted drill for 30 yards or more would take the athlete's fuel use out of the alactic system. Once the repetition is finished, rest for two to three minutes to allow for near recovery of the alactic system and thus enable maximal effort in each repetition.

Partner-resisted sprints provide a great tool not only for practicing sprint mechanics but also for producing more force in an overload aspect. The additional resistance forces the neuromuscular system to recruit more motor units (nerves and subsequent muscle fibers that it innervates) to aid in the development of more power to overcome the load. Some may think that resisted runs are as simple as tying a rope to the athlete with a tire at the end of it or having a partner maximally hold the athlete back with a resisted strap. This approach couldn't be further from the real goal, which is to mimic the exact mechanics of acceleration (chapter 7 gives fuller detail about optimal mechanics) while using resistance to slightly augment the effort without detracting from the skill performance. Too much arbitrary resistance may actually slow down limb speed for a negative training effect.

CONCLUSION

This chapter has laid to rest typical points of confusion and enabled you to think critically about your current training plan. The goal is to make training contribute to your desired end result. For example, if your art form tends toward the explosive, avoid doing too much general conditioning. On the other hand, if your discipline is more endurance based, make sure to complement your sporting needs with explosive efforts as well. The more you understand the science of sport and training, the more questions you can ask, and the better you can create effective practice approaches to enable the realization of individual athletic potential.

Now we get to the fun part: exercise selection. Chapter 5 provides a full menu of exercises to increase explosiveness and power for striking and kicking. Some of the exercises may not immediately appear to transfer to sport-specific skill sets, but the goal is to create a general environment that enables the practitioner to express his or her explosive ability and then transfer it to tactical sessions.

Exercises for Striking and Kicking

Now that we have made it through the assessment and science-based chapters, we can have a little fun with exercise selection for the next three chapters. Please note that, despite this chapter's focus on striking and kicking, the inclusion of a given exercise here does not exclude it from being a great exercise for grappling or wrestling.

Regardless of the sport, all strength and conditioning practices should follow a plan with a clearly identified starting point. To this end, many athletes, and parents of athletes, seek out my services to create a road map of sporting excellence. Usually, they already have ideas about what they need, and in most cases they gravitate toward speed or explosiveness as their top training priority. This line of thought is understandable, given that common knowledge leads them to believe that all they need to do are some explosive jumps, medicine-ball throws, Olympic lifts, or high-intensity sprints. Not so fast! In reality, we need to set the foundation first, and doing so is less about speed and explosiveness and more about stability and muscular endurance.

Imagine trying to shoot a cannon out of a canoe. This is an analogy I use with athletes who feel compelled to do only explosive exercises without laying a foundation of preparatory work. Even though the cannon itself can express explosiveness, the foundation of the canoe is unstable; it provides no solid base from which to project the cannonball. As a result, the canoe will probably tip over or be pushed forcefully backward, and the cannonball will have a dismal trajectory and projection.

The goal of strength and conditioning is to best provide the stable foundation, so that explosiveness training and power work can be done with much greater ability later in the training process. Therefore, throughout this chapter, the exercises are sequenced according to the following qualities:

- Stability and muscular endurance
- Strength
- Power
- Speed and explosiveness

STABILITY AND MUSCULAR ENDURANCE

Developing muscular endurance is a must for multiple reasons. It lays the foundation for strength and enables an athlete to maintain strength during longer events. In addition, muscular endurance and stability decrease an athlete's risk of injury. Specifically, a foundation of stability helps maintain joint integrity as a martial artist continues to throw explosive kicks and strikes in a long-lasting match.

Three Plank Positions

Equipment

None

Procedure

Lie on the floor in a forearm plank position with the palms supinated or up toward the ceiling. Attend to postural alignment by ensuring that the ears, shoulders, hips, knees, and ankles form a straight line. Then, switch to one side for the lateral plank by leaning on one elbow while stacking the feet and extending the other arm overhead. Switch sides. Hold prone (figure 5.1a) and both lateral (figure 5.1b and 5.1c) plank positions for some time, typically 20 to 45 seconds. Complete two or three sets. A given set is done once the integrity of the postural setup is lost. Signs of this loss include dropping of the hips and low back, shifting of weight, and lateral dropping of the hips. Many people hold a plank even after they have lost postural stability, which is counterproductive since stability is the most important aspect of the exercise.

Figure 5.1   Plank: (*a*) prone; (*b* and *c*) lateral.

Three-Point Pedestal

Equipment

None

Procedure

Establish good postural alignment from the ears through the shoulders, hips, knees, and ankles. Begin in full plank position with the body supported by the hands and toes (figure 5.2a). From plank position, move to one side for the lateral plank and repeat on the other side (figures 5.2b and c). Once postural alignment is disrupted, the set is done. Once the athlete can hold and maintain positions without loss of trunk control, performing leg raises is a good progression for this exercise. Complete all repetitions, typically 6-8 and each repetition must be slow and deliberate). Perform all repetitions on one side prior to switching sides. If technique suffers discontinue the leg raises.

Figure 5.2 Three-position pedestal.

Physioball Roll-Out

Equipment

Small to medium physioball

Procedure

Establish good postural alignment from the ears through the shoulders, hips, knees, and ankles. Hold a plank position with the forearms on a small- to medium-size physioball and the elbows at a 90-degree angle (figure 5.3a). Slowly roll the ball forward until the core position is about to be compromised (figure 5.3b). Pull the ball back toward the set position while driving the forearms into the ball with great intent. Perform two or three sets of 6 to 15 repetitions each and rest for 60 seconds between each set. Make it a priority to maintain a good braced hip and core position.

Figure 5.3   Physioball roll-out: (a) start position; (b) rolling ball forward.

Physioball Push-Up Hold

Equipment

Physioball

Procedure

Lie prone with the legs on a physioball and the hands on the ground directly under the shoulders. Depending on their stability, control, and strength, beginners can start with the knees on the ball, then progress to ankles on the ball, and finally to toes on the ball. Hold the body in a straight line through the ears, shoulders, hips, and knees (figure 5.4a). Begin with holds of 20 to 30 seconds for two or three sets. If the lower back becomes compromised (begins to drop), the repetition is done. Rest for 45 to 60 seconds between sets. Raising the legs one at a time during the hold is a good progression for this exercise. Complete all repetitions, typically 6-8 and each repetition must be slow and deliberate (figure 5.4b and c).

Figure 5.4   Physioball push-up hold: (a) hold position; (b and c) progression with one leg raised.

Kneeling ISO Hold

Equipment

Elastic band, stable object (e.g., weight machine)

Procedure

Attach an elastic band in a low position to a stable object. Kneel on one leg with good posture (from the hips to the shoulders to the ears) perpendicular to the band. Hold the band with the arms fully extended and resist the pull of the band (figure 5.5). Hold the position while maintaining good posture and without compensating by leaning. Hold for 20 to 30 seconds and complete two or three sets. If you cannot maintain good position, discontinue the repetition. Repeat on the other side.

Figure 5.5   Kneeling ISO hold.

Tall Monster Walk

Equipment

Elastic band

Procedure

Stand tall with an elastic band looped around the ankles. Take small lateral steps (figure 5.6). Slowly control the trailing leg, keeping it in toward the midline of the body, while maintaining a braced core. Repeat for 10 to 15 steps per lead leg. Perform two or four sets because if the athlete does three they will be imbalanced on start legs; alternate the lead leg with subsequent sets.

Figure 5.6   Tall monster walk.

Glute–Ham ISO Hold or Double-Leg Buck

Equipment

Glute–ham machine for glute–ham ISO hold or box for double-leg buck (8 to 12 inches high, or about 20 to 30 cm)

Procedure

Set up in the glute–ham machine with the hips right over the hip pad and the feet locked into the ankle pads (figure 5.7a). Use the hamstrings, glutes, and back muscles to rise to a position a little above parallel with the ground. Hold for a two-second count without overextending through the lower back (figure 5.7b). Complete six to eight repetitions, pausing for two or three seconds between repetitions. Prioritize postural alignment.

Figure 5.7   Glute–ham ISO hold (a) start position; (b) parallel position.

If you do not have access to a glute–ham machine, you can do the exercise just as effectively with a box. Lie on the ground with the knees bent 90 degrees and place both heels on the edge of the box. Drive the heels straight down into the box and slowly lift the hips. Extend fully without overextending the lower back. Perform six to eight repetitions for two or three sets while keeping the core braced. Rest for 60-90 seconds between sets.

Supine Neck Lift

When performing neck-isolation exercises, it is crucial to use good judgment. Do not add external loads for these exercises; more does *not* mean better. After performing this exercise, evaluate your soreness over the next 24 to 48 hours to determine whether a progression is needed.

Equipment

None

Procedure

Lie supine on the ground with the knees bent and the feet flat on the floor. Brace the core slightly. Press the shoulders back and down (avoid an elevated shoulder position) and press the palms firmly into the ground. Lift your head toward the ceiling without altering your chin position (figure 5.8); imagine that you are balancing a bottle on your forehead. Hold the end position for two or three seconds, then slowly lower the head back to the ground. Begin with two or three sets of five repetitions with a two-second pause between repetitions and 45 to 60 seconds of rest between sets. Progress the exercise by increasing the number of repetitions, the number of sets, or the duration of the isometric hold.

Figure 5.8   Supine neck lift.

Towel Curl to Press

Equipment

Hand towel

Procedure

Stand with the feet hip-width apart and the knees slightly bent. Hold the towel in both hands, using a firm supinated (underhand) grip with the hands at shoulder width (figure 5.9a). Pull on the towel with firm tension so that the towel is taut during the entire range of motion. Perform a biceps curl (figure 5.9b), then transition into an overhead press (figure 5.9c). Return the arms to the top of the biceps curl, then lower to the start position with the arms fully extended. Begin with two or three sets of 15 to 20 repetitions each. Rest for 45 to 60 seconds between sets. Increase the number of repetitions as muscular endurance improves.

Figure 5.9   Towel curl to press: (a) start position; (b) biceps curl; (c) overhead press.

STRENGTH

Once the foundation of muscular endurance has been laid, the athlete can work on the most important of all performance qualities—strength—which serves as the bridge to power, explosiveness, speed, and agility. The stronger the martial artist becomes, the better he or she can express the qualities needed for striking and kicking. A martial artist who builds a strong, preset foundation from muscular endurance work will possess both the repeatable speed needed to strike an opponent first and the power to do damage with each strike.

Squat

Equipment

Dumbbells, barbell (optional)

Procedure

Whatever kind of squat one performs—back, front, dumbbell, or trap-bar—this exercise is the key to strength development. As with all exercises, the top priorities in executing strength exercises must be posture and stability. Having said that, no two people squat with the same mechanics or the same range of motion. The key is to squat to a depth that you can control and that doesn't cause pain.

Typically, a squat is performed with the feet hip-width apart and flat on the ground and the toes slightly turned out. Initiate the squat by moving the hips back as if sitting back into a chair. At the same time, push the knees out and squat to the depth of comfort (figure 5.10). Perform the desired number of repetitions—usually 3 to 10 repetitions (two to five sets) for strength building, but the number may vary depending on your ultimate goal and current progress (program planning is discussed further in chapter 9).

Figure 5.10   Squat: (*a*) start position; (*b*) squatting to comfortable depth.

Flat Bench Press

The flat bench press is a horizontal pressing exercise that uses either a barbell or dumbbells to develop upper-body strength. This exercise comes in many variations; the version described here sticks with the fundamental setup and execution using a barbell.

Equipment

Flat weight bench, barbell

Procedure

Set up on the weight bench with five points of contact: both feet flat on the ground and the head, rear end, and shoulders on the weight bench. Place the hands near shoulder-width on the bar and lift the bar off of the rack using equal effort from both arms (figure 5.11a). Slowly control the bar down toward the chest (figure 5.11b). Once the bar reaches the chest, reverse direction with a pushing effort. As with the squat, each athlete has a different range of motion depending on strength, injury history, pain, and individual structural differences. Perform the desired number of repetitions—usually 3 to 10 repetitions (two to five sets) for strength building, but the number may vary depending on your ultimate goal and current progress.

Figure 5.11 Flat bench press: (a) start position; (b) lowering bar to chest.

Romanian Deadlift

This exercise helps develop strength in the legs and posterior chain, targeting muscles of the hamstrings, gluteus maximus, gastrocnemius, soleus, erector spinae latissimus dorsi, rhomboids major/minor, middle, lower and upper trapezius musculature. You can either use a barbell (as described here) or two dumbbells.

Equipment

Barbell or dumbbells

Procedure

Stand and hold the barbell with the knees slightly bent and the core braced (figure 5.12a). Hold the bar in an over-under grip (one hand pronated and the other supinated). Lower the bar slowly, brushing the thighs, until it is slightly past the slightly past the shins (figure 5.12b). Maintain a flat back. Reverse the direction of the bar by using the hamstrings; at the top of the exercise, squeeze the glutes. Perform the desired number of repetitions—usually 3 to 10 repetitions (two to five sets) for strength building, but the number may vary depending on your ultimate goal and current progress.

Figure 5.12   Romanian dead lift: (a) start position; (b) lowering bar past shins.

Push-Up and Push-Up Plus

Any push-up variation offers a great way to develop upper-body strength and endurance, but the push-up plus is a must for total body strength.

Equipment

None for push-up, medicine ball for push-up plus

Procedure

For the push-up, set up in traditional push-up position with postural alignment as the priority. Place the hands on the ground shoulder-width apart with the arms straight (figure 5.13a). Slowly lower the torso toward the ground (figure 5.13b), then reverse direction and press back to the start position while keeping the core braced. Perform the desired number of repetitions depending on the capability and training process of the athlete.

Figure 5.13 Push-up: (a) start position; (b) lowering toward the ground.

For some, the basic push-up may suffice for strength work, but for those who can complete more than 15 repetitions at a slow tempo, the exercise may be better suited for strength endurance. If that is the case, the push-up plus makes for a great progression. To perform it, place one hand on the ground and one on the medicine ball, then lower the torso to the ground (figure 5.14a). Reverse direction and return to the start position. As you finish the last degrees of range of motion, take the hand off of the ground and continue the upward push with the other hand still on the ball (figure 5.14b). Doing so challenges not only single-arm strength and stability but also the hips and core. Perform the same number of repetitions on both arms and remember to prioritize the maintenance of good body position. Perform 3 to 10 repetitions on each side for two to four sets.

Figure 5.14   Push-up plus: (a) lower toward the ground; (b) push up using only the hand on the medicine ball.

Rear-Foot Elevated Split Squat

Equipment

Bench, box, or designed rear-foot elevated roll bench; dumbbell (optional)

Procedure

Place one foot on the bench and step the other foot forward as in a lunge (figure 5.15a). Standing tall, slowly lower into a squat position while maintaining good posture (figure 5.15b). Once at the bottom of the range of motion, drive out of the squat position and finish in the extended position. Complete two to four sets of 3 to 10 repetitions, depending on where you are in your training program.

Figure 5.15   Rear-foot elevated split squat: (a) start position; (b) squat.

Split-Stance Standing Shoulder Press

A vertical press offers a great complement to horizontal presses for developing upper-body strength. For example, the split-stance standing shoulder press not only develops shoulder and upper-extremity strength but also incorporates the core.

Equipment

Flat weight bench (optional), dumbbells

Procedure

For a more advanced progression, the athlete can have one foot on a bench and the other foot flat on the ground. This forces the athlete to maintain greater tension in the core with the off-set leg positioning. Otherwise, stand with one foot in front of the other on the ground.Hold a dumbbell in each hand at shoulder height (figure 5.16a). Push the feet down into the ground and press the weights to the overhead position (figure 5.16b). Prioritize holding the correct body position throughout the hips and the core. Once the weight has been raised overhead, slowly lower to the start position, then repeat. It is ideal to perform two to four sets of 3 to 10 repetitions for strength work, but the number may vary depending on your ultimate goal and current progress

Figure 5.16 Split-stance standing shoulder press: (a) start position; (b) pressing weights overhead.

POWER

Athletes who progress their training and equip themselves with a good, broad base of strength development can in turn develop power. The more powerful a martial artist is, the quicker he or she is—and the more striking and kicking power he or she can use to gain an advantage over the opponent. As with any form of training, the limiting factor in performance transfer is the quality of an athlete's technique and execution. In other words, if an athlete sacrifices technique, he or she will miss out on the true optimization of power and increase the risk of injury.

Clean and Jerk

Equipment

Barbell or dumbbells

Procedure

Hold a pair of dumbbells, one on either side of the body, or a barbell and stand tall. Quickly drop into a squat position (figure 5.17a) and while keeping the back straight raise the bar to your knees (figure 5.17b). Then extend the hips as though jumping (figure 5.17c) while simultaneously pulling the barbell or dumbbells to the catch position (figure 5.17d). Once stable in the catch position, drop into the quarter-squat position (figure 5.17e) and quickly extend the hips while driving the barbell or dumbbells overhead (figure 5.17f). This is an advanced skill that takes time to learn. For best power output, perform three to five sets of one to five repetitions, depending on where you are in your training program.

Figure 5.17 Clean and jerk: (a) squat position; (b) raising the barbell to the knees.

Figure 5.17   Clean and jerk: (*c*) extending the hips; (*d*) pulling barbell to catch position; (*e*) quarter-squat position; (*f*) driving barbell overhead.

Landmine Row to Punch

Equipment

Barbell and weight plates, or landmine device

Procedure

Place one end of the barbell either in a corner of the room or flat on the weight room floor, or use a landmine device as shown. Stand perpendicular to the bar with the legs staggered; the leg opposite the working arm is in front. Firmly grip the fat part of the barbell (figure 5.18a). Brace the core and row with one arm (figure 5.18b). Swiftly transition the bar to the other arm in a punching motion (figure 5.18c) and reposition the feet so that they are parallel to the bar (figure 5.18d). Carefully lower the bar to the ground. Perform two or three sets of three to five repetitions per side. As technique is mastered, increase the speed of the action as long as you are able to hold the braced core position through the row and transition to the punch.

Figure 5.18   Landmine row to punch: (a) grip the barbell; (b) row; (c) punch; (d) reposition the feet.

Plyometric Push-Up

Equipment

Weight plate, flat weight bench for variation

Procedure

Depending on ability, this exercise can be done in several ways. The advanced exercise starts on the ground in a push-up position with a weight plate between the hands (figure 5.19a). Rapidly descend (figure 5.19b) and then ascend with force to propel the torso as high as possible (figure 5.19c). Catch with both hands on the weight plate (figure 5.19d) and rapidly descend into a narrow push-up. Quickly reverse position to extension of the arms and ascend again while moving the hands back to the ground. Thus one repetition equals one complete cycle: push-up from ground to weight plate followed by push-up from weight plate to ground. Maintain a braced core for each repetition and perform two or three sets of three to eight repetitions. This sequence of work allows you to express good power and harness the skill of the exercise; the timing can be tricky but is essential in order to maximize power.

Figure 5.19   Plyometric push-up: (a) start position; (b) descending into lower push-up position; (c) ascending with force and lifting the torso; (d) catching the hands on the weight plate.

Variation

For a good modification of the plyometric push-up, set up at an angle on a weight bench. This setup decreases the total weight that the upper extremity must push away and allows the athlete to produce more speed than is possible in a traditional push-up position. This variation does not use the weight plate; instead, forcefully ascend to lift the hands off of the weight bench, then catch on the bench again.

Hip Thrust

Equipment

Flat weight bench, barbell

Procedure

The hip thrust is a good exercise to load the legs while decreasing the load on the spine. Set up in a supine position with the shoulder blades on a weight bench and a barbell at the hip crease with both knees bent (figure 5.20a). Drive up through the heels and extend the hips maximally with good speed and without overextending through the back (figure 5.20b). Slowly lower the weight and repeat. It suffices to perform two or three sets of three to six repetitions, but the numbers may vary depending on where you are in your training program.

Figure 5.20 Hip thrust: (a) start position; (b) hip extension.

Variation

For someone who is not quite ready to load with weight, a nice variation is to perform a single-leg hip thrust (figure 5.21). This variation can still be a challenging exercise since one leg does the work. Do not use the barbell. Make sure that hip position stays level from side to side as you move from hip flexion to hip extension.

Figure 5.21 Single-leg hip thrust: (*a*) start position; (*b*) hip thrust.

Medicine-Ball Jam

This is a fantastic exercise for developing upper-body power in extension (as in a strike) and for complementing shoulder-integrity work.

Equipment

Medicine ball (preferably sand filled)

Procedure

Grab a medicine ball (preferably sand filled as it will provide more stability for the exercise) with both hands and hold it in an extended position while in a narrow push-up position (figure 5.22a). Descend rapidly and bring the chest to the ball (figure 5.22b). Reverse direction explosively and ascend as high as possible (figure 5.22c). For those with good upper-body power, it is not uncommon for the ball to leave the ground. However, the real beauty of the exercise lies in the stability that is needed once you and the ball return to the ground. At impact, maintain a braced core and stay stable through the shoulders. Keep repetitions in the range of three to six for two or three sets, depending on where you are in your training program.

Figure 5.22 Medicine-ball jam: (a) start position; (b) descending and bringing chest to ball; (c) ascending explosively as high as possible.

Sled Push

Use sled pushes to develop good lower-body power. The same exercise can be done for lower-body endurance by varying the amount of time used for each repetition and the amount of recovery time.

Equipment

Sled with weights

Procedure

For developing power, use 6 to 10 seconds per sprint and maximize recovery by resting for two to three minutes between repetitions. Use good sprint posture and proper running mechanics (figure 5.23). Your intent during the exercise must be to drive through the ground and fully extend the hips for maximal power. Perform two or three sets of two to four repetitions, depending on your training level and goals.

Figure 5.23   Sled push.

Suspension Training Sled Row or Suspension Training Inverted Row

Equipment

Suspension training straps, weighted sled

Procedure

Attach the TRX, or other suspension machine, to a weighted sled. While maintaining a squat position, pull the handles through the mid-section forcefully while explosively driving the hips into extension (figure 5.24). As the sled moves, step back and reset in the squat position. Perform three to six repetitions, depending on where you are in your programming.

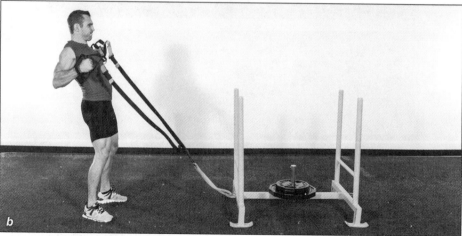

Figure 5.24   Sled row.

Figure 5.24 *(continued)* Sled row.

If you do not have access to a sled, perform inverted rows with a suspension trainer. Set the device so that you can get into a horizontal position parallel to the floor (ultimately, the angle depends on individual strength). The stronger you are, the better you will be able to perform the exercise from a horizontal position. Modify the angle as needed to complete all the repetitions. Prioritize postural alignment and keep the core tight. Row with speed and hold at the top of the range of motion for a one- or two-second count. Complete two or three sets of the desired number of repetitions, depending on program goals and current progress.

SPEED AND EXPLOSIVENESS

Now that the martial artist has been exposed to high-quality strength and power work, he or she can use speed and explosiveness exercises to complete the package. Returning to the analogy of the cannon and the canoe, the athlete can now shoot the cannonball from a more stable environment, which means more speed!

Sprints

Equipment

Running track

Procedure

Speed and explosiveness can best be expressed in sprinting. More specifically, sprinting for 10, 20, and 30 yards (or meters) tends to yield the best use of total body explosiveness muscles and the alactic energy system. Different start positions make great variations for practicing reacting from different sport positions, but to best express sprint ability the two-point start (figure 5.25) is ideal as the athlete is beginning from the most efficient and optimal starting point to have successful mechanics. Attack each distance with maximal effort while staying relaxed to make best use of muscle elasticity. With every repetition, alternate lead legs at the start to avoid overuse injury. Perform two or three sets of three or four repetitions.

Figure 5.25   Two-point start for sprints.

Overhead Medicine-Ball Throw

Equipment

Medicine ball (4 to 15 pounds, or 2 to 6 kilograms)

Procedure

Hold the medicine ball overhead with the arms fully extended (figure 5.26a). Rapidly drop to a squat position and bring the ball between the knees (figure 5.26b). Explosively reverse direction to stand and jump with maximal effort, throwing the ball behind you (figure 5.26c). Perform two or three sets of two to five repetitions, depending on where you are in the training program.

Figure 5.26 Overhead medicine-ball throw: (a) start position; (b) squatting and bringing ball between knees; (c) jumping and throwing ball behind.

Medicine-Ball Rotational Throw

Equipment

Medicine ball, wall

Procedure

Stand perpendicular to a reinforced wall with the feet farther than hip-width apart (figure 5.27a). Hold a medicine ball with both hands. Load your weight onto the inside edge of the outside foot. Push into the ground to produce rotation from the legs, hips, trunk, and shoulders while the arms serve to carry the ball into the wall (figure 5.27b). Do not just throw the ball with the arms and hands; use the entire body. Complete two or three sets of three to five repetitions on each side; modify these numbers as necessary based on program goals and progress.

Figure 5.27   Medicine-ball rotational throw: (a) start position; (b) rotating ball into wall.

Dumbbell Squat Jump

Equipment

Light dumbbells

Procedure

Use light dumbbells for a slight (5 to 10 percent) overload of body weight. Stand tall with the feet hip-width apart (figure 5.28a). Quickly drop into a squat position (figure 5.28b) and jump explosively as high as possible (figure 5.28c). Land in a squat position. Perform two or three sets of three to five repetitions, depending on programming.

Figure 5.28 Dumbbell squat jump: (a) start position; (b) dropping into squat position; (c) jumping as high as possible.

Partner Medicine-Ball Drop

Equipment

Box (12 to 20 inches high, or 30 to 50 centimeters), medicine ball (6.5 to 17.5 pounds, or 3 to 8 kilograms), partner

Procedure

Lie on the floor with a partner standing on the box over you. The partner drops the medicine ball over your chest (figure 5.29a). Catch it first and quickly lower the ball to your chest (figure 5.29b), then forcefully drive the ball back up to the partner (figure 5.29c). The ball is relatively light, so use massive intent regarding speed of movement. Perform two or three sets of three to eight repetitions (modify these numbers if necessary).

Figure 5.29 Partner medicine-ball drop: (a) Drop medicine ball to partner; (b) catch and lower medicine ball to chest; (c) drive ball back up to partner.

Overhead Medicine-Ball Slam

Equipment

Medicine ball (6 to 12 lb, or 3 to 6 kg)

Procedure

Stand tall with the arms overhead while holding the medicine ball (figure 5.30a). The feet are hip-width apart and the knees are slightly bent. Brace the core. Violently drive the arms down toward the ground. Release the ball (figure 5.30b) and follow through with the arms past the hips. Perform two or three sets of three to six repetitions, depending on programming.

Figure 5.30 Overhead medicine-ball slam: (a) start position; (b) driving arms and ball to the ground.

CONCLUSION

Bruce Lee once said, "I fear not the man who has practiced 10,000 kicks once. But I fear the man who has practiced one kick 10,000 times." This distinction can hold true for strength and conditioning.

This chapter showed you 30 exercises for kicking and striking, and honestly that is more than enough. Thousands of variations are available, but ultimately it comes down to how well the exercises are done and with what intent. Are stability-based exercises done with perfect posture? Are explosive exercises done at the appropriate speed? Are all the other qualities of training being done with the proper set-and-repetition scheme, as well as adequate rest to maximize ability? Accountability must be placed on the athlete to adhere to the technique and structure of training if she or he wants to maximize individual potential.

Chapter 6

Exercises for Wrestling and Grappling

As discussed in chapter 5, there is no single perfect exercise or routine for any given area of martial arts. For example, some exercises are great for grappling and also carry benefits for striking. Likewise, an exercise that seems very specific to striking can provide massive transfer to wrestling. As a result, we must avoid pigeonholing the programming, and many exercises presented here can help athletes whose chosen discipline lacks a grappling or wrestling component.

Aside from pure skill, specific abilities can make someone a much more effective grappler. Consider, for example, the qualities of strength: Superior endurance, explosiveness, and pure strength give an athlete the upper hand if he or she is competing against someone with a similar skill set for takedowns, throws, and submissions. The mechanics of such moves mean that certain strength qualities change an athlete's ability to execute them. With this relationship in mind, a training program must address lower-body strength and power, upper-body pulling, grip strength, and core strength.

The exercises presented here are divided into the categories of stability and endurance, strength, power, speed, and explosiveness. This progression ensures that all strength bases are covered and that all training levels enable success and offer plenty of exercises to choose from.

STABILITY AND ENDURANCE

Stability and endurance are critical for wrestlers and grapplers. They set the foundation for building strength and power during the training process, and they enable better transfer to the strength and power needed in sport performance, especially as fatigue sets in. Much of the sport performance in this case involves clinch positions that require pushing and pulling actions while maintaining a good base of support for seconds or even minutes at a time. Great muscular endurance helps an athlete outlast the opponent late in the match while fighting for a takedown or submission.

In addition, good stability in the shoulders, core, trunk, hips, and legs keeps the athlete healthier during training. This is particularly true of grappling, in which many positions challenge the end ranges of motion (where injury is more likely). Therefore, working on this specific quality of stability helps the martial artist avoid common pathologies associated with the shoulders, back, knees, and hips. No training plan is foolproof, but the goal is to provide the necessary stress on the athlete to make him or her more bulletproof when engaged in harmful positions associated with martial arts.

Elbow Tap

Equipment

None

Procedure

Begin in a push-up position with the hands slightly less than shoulder-width apart and the feet slightly farther apart than the hips (figure 6.1a). To maximize the stabilizing effort, brace the core and push into the ground with the balls of the feet and the palms. Slowly take one hand off of the ground and tap the opposite elbow without losing hip or spinal positioning (figure 6.1b). Perform two or three sets of six to eight taps per side; stop if good position can no longer be held. The tempo should be slow and deliberate in order to maximize endurance and technique.

Figure 6.1 Elbow tap: (a) start in push-up position; (b) tap opposite elbow.

Toe Tap

Equipment

None

Procedure

Begin in a push-up position with the hands slightly less than shoulder-width apart and the feet slightly farther apart than the hips (figure 6.2a). To maximize muscular tensions, brace the core and push into the ground with the balls of the feet and the palms. Simultaneously move one hand and the opposite foot toward each other and tap the foot with the hand (figure 6.2b). Slowly replace the hand and the foot, then repeat on the other side. Perform two or three sets of three to eight taps per side; stop if good positioning can no longer be held. The tempo of the exercise must be slow and deliberate in order to maximize endurance and technique.

Figure 6.2   Toe tap: (a) start in push-up position; (b) move one hand and the opposite foot toward each other and tap the foot with the hand.

Physioball Partner Push

Equipment

Physioball, partner

Procedure

Begin in an athletic position. Clinch a physioball between the hands. Maintain a flat back. Push the feet into the ground for a stable base. Brace the core as your partner pushes on the ball from multiple directions (figure 6.3), forcing you to react and stabilize. Continue for 20 to 45 seconds; perform two or three sets.

Figure 6.3   Physioball partner push.

Stir the Pot

Equipment

Small physioball

Procedure

Begin in a plank position with the forearms parallel on a small physioball. While keeping the core braced, put pressure into the ball with the forearms and slowly rotate clockwise and counterclockwise for five repetitions in each direction (figure 6.4). Perform two or three sets without losing hip or spinal position.

Figure 6.4   Stir the pot.

Battle-Rope Drumming

Equipment

Battle ropes

Procedure

Stand in an athletic position and hold the battle ropes firmly. Begin an alternating drumming pattern with the arms (figure 6.5). Brace the core and hold the shoulders down and back for greater stability. Perform this exercise for 10 to 15 seconds and three to five sets. As work capacity increases, increase the time and set numbers as long as technique is not sacrificed.

Figure 6.5   Battle-rope drumming.

Battle-Rope Fly

Equipment

Battle ropes

Procedure

Stand in an athletic position and hold the battle ropes firmly with a thumb-up grip. Begin a simultaneous lateral flying pattern with the arms (figure 6.6). Brace the core and hold the shoulders down and back for greater stability. Perform this exercise for 10 to 15 seconds and repeat for three to five sets. As work capacity increases, increase the time and set numbers as long as technique is not sacrificed.

Figure 6.6 Battle-rope fly.

STRENGTH

Aside from technical ability, strength is the most critical factor for throwing, sweeping, reversing, escaping, or submitting the opponent. Therefore, a martial artist needs to develop total-body strength through the training program. In particular, if a martial artist develops superior upper-body push and pull, as well as lower body and trunk strength, then he or she holds the advantage over opponents both on the feet and on the ground.

In addition to doing typical strength exercises, great wrestlers and grapplers can separate themselves from the rest of the pack by training for neck and grip strength. Therefore, the following presentation of traditional strength exercises includes variations to aid the development of these qualities in order to build unstoppable grapplers and wrestlers.

In this section, strength and power are closely related. What separates these training qualities is the amount of weight used; in other words, you can adjust the weight (load) to emphasize either strength or power with the same exercise. To emphasize strength, use a weight that is close to maximal load (85 percent of 1-repetition max, or 1RM) for five repetitions; to emphasize power, lower the load (30 to 60 percent of 1RM) for five repetitions and add speed to the exercise. These options allow you to make better choices regarding sets, repetitions, and loads depending on the competition calendar. In addition, regardless of whether or not one competes, it is critical to adjust loads to make long-term training sustainable by minimizing burnout and overtraining.

Deadlift

Equipment

Barbell

Procedure

The deadlift comes in many variations and is not a one-size-fits-all exercise. Some people have no problem advancing into the start position. However, depending on limb length, flexibility, and injury history, some people should modify this exercise or avoid it completely.

To perform the exercise, begin in a deep squat position with the feet slightly outside hip width. Grasp the bar with an over–under grip between the knees. With both feet flat on the ground, fully extend the arms so that the shoulders are down (figure 6.7a) and the back stays flat. Initiate the pull by pushing the feet into the ground while bracing the core. Lift the bar, maintaining the bar path next to the shins. Drive the hips through the bar to the standing position while maximally squeezing the glutes (figure 6.7b). As you lower the bar, maintain bar contact on the thighs and shins. Slightly hinge the hips back and sit down into a squat while maintaining a braced core. Perform three to six sets of three to five repetitions, depending on programming.

Figure 6.7   Deadlift: (a) over–under grip of the bar and extending the arms; (b) initiating the pull and lifting the bar past the knees.

Bent-Over Row

Equipment

Barbell

Procedure

Start in an athletic position with the feet hip-width apart and the knees slightly bent. Bend at the waist while maintaining a flat back and a braced core. Grasp the barbell in either an overhand or an underhand grip (figure 6.8a). Row the barbell toward the midsection of the torso without breaking postural position (figure 6.8b). Perform two to five sets of three to eight repetitions.

Figure 6.8 Bent-over row: (a) start position; (b) rowing barbell toward torso.

Landmine Row

Equipment

Barbell, weight plate of 5, 10, or 25 pounds (about 2, 5, or 10 kg); or landmine device

Procedure

Place one end of the barbell either in the corner of the room between two walls or flat on the weight room floor, or use a landmine device. Stand perpendicular toward one end of the barbell with one leg forward—the leg opposite the arm that will be rowing. Firmly grip the fat part of the barbell (figure 6.9a), brace the core, and slowly row the barbell to your side without breaking the plane of the back (figure 6.9b). Slowly lower the barbell to the start position. Perform two or three sets of five to eight repetitions.

Figure 6.9   Landmine row: (a) start position; (b) rowing.

Pull-Up

Equipment

Pull-up bar

Procedure

The pull-up is one of the best exercises for developing total upper-body strength. It also improves grip strength and shoulder integrity.

Grab a pull-up bar with a preferred grip—wide, narrow, underhand, neutral, or overhand. Generally, the neutral and underhand grips are best for beginners and for people who are challenged in upper-body strength, whereas the overhand and wide grips should be used by people with more training time and upper-body strength. In any case, use a grip that allows you to travel through the range of motion without pain.

If you are a beginner, start with a slight elbow bend; if you are stronger, begin with the elbows straight, as long as you feel no pain. The legs are bent or crossed at the ankles (figure 6.10a). Slowly pull up until you reach full range (figure 6.10b) and your chin goes over the bar. Slowly descend to the fully extended position at the elbows. Complete three to five sets of three to eight repetitions.

Figure 6.10   Pull-up: (a) start position; (b) pulling up to full range.

Variation

As strength grows, a variety of grips can be used. For example, fat grips and towels are just a couple of variations that challenge grip strength. For better wrist control and hand-fighting ability, using fat grips simulates the girth of an opponent's forearms and challenges the grip in weaker positions than how it is challenged with a normal bar. If you do not have fat grips, use a towel draped over the bar and clinch both ends as a cheap and effective substitute to simulate greater girth. The limiting factor in these exercises is usually the grip, so it is very important to implement these strategies every so often to avoid losing strength in the arms and the back.

Walking Lunge

Equipment

Dumbbells (optional)

Procedure

Depending on ability, either use simple body weight or add dumbbells for more resistance. If using dumbbells, either hold one dumbbell in the goblet position under the chin or hold two dumbbells at the sides. Stand with the feet together (figure 6.11a). Take a forward step and slowly lower into a lunge position. Pause at the bottom without letting the back knee touch the ground (figure 6.11b). The lead foot must stay flat, and the posture must stay upright. Using the lead leg, push out of the lunge position and bring the rear leg to the standing position. Perform two to four sets of five to eight repetitions per leg.

Figure 6.11 Walking lunge: (a) start position; (b) lunge position.

Single-Arm Dumbbell Row

Equipment

Dumbbell, weight bench

Procedure

Stand with the feet staggered. Place one hand on a weight bench and brace the core. Hold a dumbbell in the other hand with the arm straight (figure 6.12a). Slowly pull the dumbbell up to the torso (figure 6.12b), then slowly return it to the start position. Complete three to five sets of three to eight repetitions on each arm.

Figure 6.12   Single-arm dumbbell row: (a) start position; (b) lift dumbbell up to torso.

Farmer Walk

Equipment

Dumbbells

Procedure

Stand tall while holding a dumbbell in each hand at the side. Slowly walk as tall as possible while bracing the core and pinching the shoulders back (figure 6.13). This action challenges grip strength, shoulder and hip strength, and core strength. Perform the exercise for 45 to 60 seconds for two or three sets. As strength increases, increase the number of sets and the time per repetition.

Figure 6.13   Farmer walk.

Heavy-Bag Carry

Equipment

Heavy bag (30 to 140 pounds, or about 14 to 64 kg)

Procedure

Prop the bag in an upright position. Keeping the back flat, bend at the knees in front of the bag and place your arms around the bag as if doing a bear hug (figure 6.14a). Lock the hands with a Gable grip: palms perpendicular but facing each other and fingers wrapped around the back of the opposite hand. Once the grip is locked in, brace the core and lift through the legs to a full standing position (figure 6.14b). Walk forward slowly while maximally squeezing the grip and the bag. Once the repetition is over, slowly lower the bag while bending the knees. Each repetition should last 20 to 30 seconds; as strength increases, increase the duration of the repetition. Complete two or three sets.

Figure 6.14 Heavy-bag carry: (a) start position; (b) and carry.

Fat-Grip Horizontal Row

Equipment

TRX or other suspension device, fat-grip accessories, mounting that allows you to be parallel to the floor, 12- to 16-inch (30 to 40 cm) box (optional)

Procedure

Set the suspension device at a height that allows full arm extension without the back touching the ground. Depending on strength, set up with the feet firmly on the ground or on the box so that the body is parallel to the ground. Place the hands, including the thumbs, firmly around the fat grips and brace the core (figure 6.15a). Perform a rowing action, bringing the chest toward the ceiling and the elbows to the plane of the back, while maximizing the squeeze of the grip and emphasizing the muscles of the back at the top of the range of motion (figure 6.15b). Slowly lower back to the fully extended position, then repeat. Perform two or three sets of five to eight repetitions.

As strength increases, try pausing at the top position. Doing so challenges the grip longer through the set and challenges the athlete to isometrically hold the most difficult position in the exercise. An athlete is only as strong as her or his weakest link.

Figure 6.15   Fat-grip horizontal row: (a) start position; (b) rowing.

POWER

Power is defined as the rate of doing work. Power and strength are similar qualities, but power involves a time component that makes it more specific. This distinction is the reason that percentage of load matters. We can influence power by moving a large mass (i.e., exerting force); however, it will be moved slowly. Alternatively, we can influence power by moving a lighter mass with more speed (i.e., achieving velocity). Managing these variables involves manipulating what is referred to as the force–velocity relationship. Ultimately, the many subcategories of strength come down to this relationship: how much load is used and how fast it is moved.

Zercher Squat

Equipment

Barbell

Procedure

Stand with the feet slightly farther than hip-width apart. Hold the barbell at the elbows in the crease of the biceps (figure 6.16a). Keep the weight lighter than that used in a traditional squat workout (50 to 60 percent of 1RM). Slowly descend into a squat (figure 6.16b), then ascend with strong intent to achieve speed while maintaining a braced core. Perform three to five sets of three to six repetitions.

Figure 6.16 Zercher squat: (a) start position; (b) descent into squat.

Horizontal-Pull Explosive Regrip

Equipment

Barbell, rack, mat (or pad)

Procedure

Lie beneath a barbell that is racked at a low position. Begin with the body at a 45-degree angle and the hands gripping the bar in either an overhand or an underhand grip. Keep the arms fully extended (figure 6.17a). Explosively pull the torso toward the bar, release the hands from the bar (figure 6.17b), and quickly regrip the bar and hold at the top. Return slowly to the extended position (figure 6.17c), then repeat (figure 6.17d). Complete two to four sets of three to eight repetitions.

Figure 6.17   Horizontal-pull explosive regrip: (a) start position; (b) releasing hands from bar; (c) return to the extended position; (d) repeat.

Single-Leg Box Blast

Equipment

Plyometric box (6 to 8 in., or 15 to 20 cm)

Procedure

Stand with the feet staggered—one foot forward on the plyometric box, the other behind on the ground and the arms extended overhead (figure 6.18*a*). Lower into a squat position (figure 6.18*b*), then explode vertically with both legs (figure 6.18*c*). Complete two to four sets of three to five repetitions per leg.

Figure 6.18   Single-leg box blast: (*a*) start position; (*b*) descent to squat; (*c*) upward explosion with both legs.

Physioball Cable Rotation

Equipment

Physioball, cable machine with handle attachment

Procedure

Hold the physioball at chest height, pinching it between the arms. Stand in an athletic position sideways to the cable machine. Hold the handle of the cable machine in the far arm at sternum height (figure 6.19*a*). Rotate the torso (figure 6.19*b*) evenly on both sides (figure 6.19*c*) while maintaining a braced core. Perform two to four sets of five to eight repetitions per side.

Figure 6.19   Physioball cable rotation: (*a*) start position; (*b* and *c*) torso rotation.

Open-Stance Medicine-Ball Throw

Equipment

Reinforced wall, medicine ball weighing 4 to 18 pounds (about 2 to 8 kg) depending on strength

Procedure

Face a reinforced wall in an open position with the knees slightly bent or in an athletic position. Hold the medicine ball in both hands at hip height. Push both feet firmly into the ground and rotate one shoulder back to stretch the rotators of the trunk (figure 6.20a). Rapidly rotate the shoulder back to the wall and throw the medicine ball (figure 6.20b). Aggressively push the feet into the ground while rapidly rotating the shoulders to the wall in order to link the kinetic chain from the feet to the hands, thereby increasing the speed of movement. Perform two or three sets of six to eight repetitions on each side.

The number of repetitions for this exercise is slightly higher than most power and speed exercises because the load is very light and because it typically takes about three repetitions to find the needed rhythm and timing. Thus, the specified number of repetitions provides a chance to adjust before increasing the speed. As technical proficiency and speed improve, increase the weight of the medicine ball.

Figure 6.20   Open-stance medicine-ball throw: (a) start position; (b) throw.

Closed-Stance Medicine-Ball Throw

Equipment

Reinforced wall, medicine ball weighing 4 to 18 pounds (about 2 to 8 kg) depending on strength

Procedure

Stand perpendicular to the wall in a slightly athletic position with the knees slightly bent and the feet hip-width apart. Hold the medicine ball in both hands in front of the legs (figure 6.21a). Simultaneously shift your weight to the outside leg so that the inside leg lifts off of the ground (as when a baseball pitcher throws the ball) and shift the ball back toward the outside leg (figure 6.21b). Push through the ground to elicit an extension-and-rotation response that starts at the foot and moves up through the legs and hips to finish through the trunk and shoulders as you release the ball into the wall (figure 6.21c). Perform two or three sets of six to eight repetitions. Adjust the number of repetitions and sets as needed based on programming goals and objectives.

Figure 6.21   Closed-stance medicine-ball throw: (a) start position; (b) loading of outside leg; (c) throw.

Glute–Ham Raise

Equipment

Glute–ham bench

Procedure

Start on the glute–ham bench with the trunk flexed over the hip pad. Start at a 90-degree angle at the hips and torso (figure 6.22a). Raise the torso until parallel with legs (figure 6.22b) and then drive the legs into a 90-degree angle at the knees (figure 6.22c) without losing core stability to maximize activation of the hamstrings and gluteus maximus. Complete three sets of five repetitions.

The stronger you are, the less distance from the hip pad to the foot placement. However, if you are breaking core position to finish the exercise, then your core may be the weak link in the chain, in which case a regression of the exercise should be performed. Hold a 180-degree position isometrically or start in the finish position with 90-degree angles at the knee joints and slowly lower into the 180-degree position.

Figure 6.22   Glute–ham raise: (a) start position; (b) parallel with legs; (c) 90-degree angle at knees.

Medicine-Ball Broad Jump

Equipment

Medicine ball

Procedure

Start in a tall position with the feet hip-width apart. Hold a medicine ball at chest height (figure 6.23a). Rapidly drop into a squat position (figure 6.23b), then jump explosively and drive the medicine ball forward, throwing it with as much power as possible (figure 6.23c) and land (figure 6.23d). Complete three to five sets of three to five repetitions.

Figure 6.23 Medicine-ball broad jump: (a) start position; (b) squat; (c) jumping and driving the medicine ball forward; (d) land.

SPEED AND EXPLOSIVENESS

Speed and explosiveness are major keys to defending takedown attempts, passing the guard, attempting takedowns, and sinking in a submission. Building on power, speed and explosiveness lie at the extreme end of the force–velocity curve. Therefore, most of the exercises presented here use only body weight, and the goal in performing them is to orchestrate the body to move as fast as possible.

Burpee

Equipment

Medicine ball (optional)

Procedure

Begin in a standing position. Quickly squat and kick the legs into a push-up position (figure 6.24, *a* and *b*). Just as quickly, pull the knees back to the chest and explode back to the standing position (figure 6.24, *c* and *d*). Complete two or three sets of six to eight repetitions. Remember that the goal of the movement is not conditioning but speed. Burpees provide a great tool that often gets lumped into conditioning only, but they offer one of the best speed drills for wresters and grapplers. This rationale explains the relatively limited number of sets and repetitions for these exercises as compared with the numbers used in conditioning circuits.

Figure 6.24   Burpee: (*a*) start position; (*b*) kicking legs out to push-up position; (*c*) pulling knees back to chest; (*d*) standing up.

Partner Reactive Shuffle

Equipment

Partner

Procedure

Start in an athletic position facing the partner. If training with a coach, he or she indicates the direction in which to shuffle. If training with a partner, the partner shuffles with you. Shuffle quickly as your partner provides a change-of-direction stimulus, such as clapping or mirroring (figure 6.25a through d). Do not cross your feet as you shuffle; do maintain athletic position. Continue for only six to eight seconds since the goal is not aerobic conditioning but quickness. Perform three to five sets.

Figure 6.25   Partner reactive shuffle.

Figure 6.25 *(continued)*

Push-Up Sprint

Equipment

Partner

Procedure

Start in a prone position (figure 6.26a). On the coach's or partner's command, explode from the ground (figure 6.26b) and sprint (figure 6.26c) as fast as possible for 10 yards (or meters). Perform two or three sets of four or five repetitions (one 10-yard run is one repetition). The goal is to minimize fatigue but maximize speed and quickness.

Figure 6.26 Push-up sprint: (a) start position; (b) exploding from the ground; (c)sprint.

Get-Up

Equipment

Partner

Procedure

Start in a supine position (on the back) with the knees bent and the feet flat (figure 6.27a). On a coach's or partner's command, explode to the feet in an offensive position (figure 6.27b). Focus on footwork each time you return to your feet. Repeat for three to five sets of six to eight repetitions.

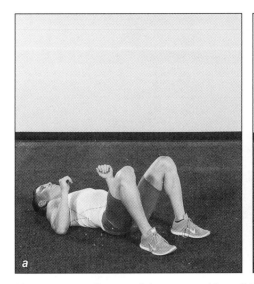

Figure 6.27   Get-up: (a) start position; (b) offensive position.

Hip Rotation

Equipment

Agility ladder (optional)

Procedure

Stand in a low athletic position (figure 6.28a). While staying in place, rotate the hips as quickly as possible while keeping the core braced (figure 6.28b). The feet move with the hips. Repeat for six to eight seconds for two or three sets with full rest between sets to allow complete recovery and maximize speed in each repetition.

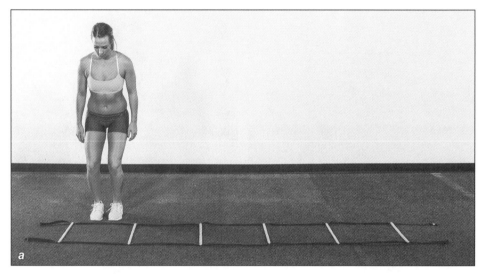

Figure 6.28 Hip rotation: (a) start position; (b) quick hip rotation.

In and Out

Equipment

Agility ladder (optional)

Procedure

Stand in an athletic position with the feet narrowly spaced. Quickly move the feet in (figure 6.29*a*) and out (figure 6.29*b*) at maximal speed for six to eight seconds for two or three sets. Allow a full recovery between sets to enable maximal speed in each repetition.

Figure 6.29　In and out: (*a*) feet in; (*b*) feet out.

Lateral In and Outs

Equipment

Agility ladder (optional)

Procedure

Stand in athletic position with feet about hip width apart. Step forward with the lead leg either in a ladder or using a line on a court or field (closest to the direction the athlete is going) and immediately follow with the trail leg (see figure 6.30). Repeat with maximal speed for four repetitions of six to eight seconds for 2 to 3 sets.

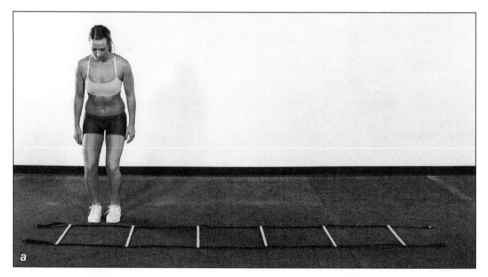

Figure 6.30   Lateral in and outs.

Figure 6.30 *(continued)* Lateral in and outs.

CONCLUSION

For some exercises, the transferability to sport is not immediately obvious. As a result, one of the most common mistakes made by practitioners involves trying to force each exercise to exhibit the outward appearance of the skill for which the athlete is training. To avoid this mistake, remember that the goal is to make the athlete as strong, stable, powerful, and explosive as possible so that he or she can best express his or her individual skill set.

Variation of training stressors (sets, reps, load, and exercise selection) is the key because it challenges the body's ability to adapt to a new stressor while decreasing overuse injuries. We are looking for adaptation in training, not accommodation. Early on, the routine is about learning specific exercises correctly; once learned, the athlete can add more load or greater speed to a given exercise so the body can recover and adapt to the new stress. Yes, variation can help offset boredom, but more importantly the training response of novel tasks is what helps the body adapt to a new ability.

Variation of the training stressors is the key as the athlete becomes more consistent with the training routine. Even for a striking discipline, the grappling and wrestling exercises are great exercises to include in a training program as many of the strength qualities transfer over from stability, strength, power, and speed; similarly, if the chosen sport is more grappling based, striking exercises still aid the athlete's abilities.

The next chapter addresses speed and agility, which makes this book unique. Most martial arts books focus on warm-ups, strength, and flexibility while treating speed and agility as automatic benefits of all the other work. However, movement is the key to all sports, and the next chapter shows you how to develop the speed and agility that transfer to the needs of the chosen sport. The goal is to provide the best drills to maximize the skill and avoid drills that offer little or no transfer. The intent and precision that characterize the chapter enable you to take athleticism to the next level of performance!

Chapter 7

Exercises for Speed and Agility

As mentioned earlier, speed is the X factor in sport performance. At the same time, it is influenced by other factors. In fact, many of the trainable qualities—endurance, strength, power, flexibility, balance, and coordination—contribute to the development of both speed and agility.

Chapters 5 and 6 present exercises that contribute to speed and agility. This chapter, in turn, provides a technical perspective on those exercises. Speed training should not be confused with conditioning. Too often, both athletes and coaches blur these lines and therefore fail to train for pure speed. Incorporating such training into a program is covered in depth in chapter 9 (Program Planning and Periodization for Martial Arts). For now, it is sufficient to understand that this type of training should be done at a point during the training week when the athlete is fresh and recovered.

At first glance, many of the drills presented here may seem as if they could be found at the local track or football field and might not seem like an exercise for martial artists. However, that's fine because of the real benefits they provide. The beauty of this type of training is that it makes the martial artist more explosive and agile, thus allowing for better transfer of athleticism on the mat. The big-picture goals here are to make the athlete more explosive, to train the nervous system to fire faster, and to help the athlete learn to orchestrate fast limb movements that carry great power.

SPEED

Acceleration is the rate at which speed is increased. Many factors determine an athlete's ability to accelerate, including genetics, leverage characteristics, and relative strength—that is, how strong the athlete is in relation to his or her body weight. Relative strength is the most important factor, and it can be measured by the vertical jump and broad jump tests used in chapter 2 to measure lower-body power and explosiveness.

Even when an athlete is gifted with the genetics that help make a person lightning fast, he or she can do many things on the technical side to get even faster and to decrease the likelihood of injury. From a technical perspective, martial artists don't need to train like sprinters. They do, however, need to work on a few drills that help them become faster and more explosive in using their chosen skill set.

ACCELERATION WALL DRILLS

All wall-drill exercises begin in the same setup position. Stand facing a wall and lean into the wall (or other stable surface) at a 45- to 60-degree angle with both hands on the wall. Maintain alignment from the ears to the ankles with your body weight driving through the balls of the feet into the ground.

Wall Drill One-Count

Equipment

Wall, partner

Procedure

Assume the setup position for the wall drill (figure 7.1a). Start with one leg up in 75 degrees of hip flexion with the knee bent slightly less than 90 degrees and the foot in the dorsiflexed (toe-up) position. The down leg should be straight with the weight driving through the ball of the foot. Brace the core. On a coach's or partner's command, quickly punch the down leg to the up position and drive the up leg to the down position without breaking postural position in the core and back (figure 7.1b). Return to the start position. Perform 10 repetitions (five per leg). Rest for 60 seconds, then repeat; do three sets.

Figure 7.1   Wall drill one-count: (*a*) start position; (*b*) leg up.

Wall Drill Two-Count

Equipment

Wall, partner

Procedure

Assume the setup position for the wall drill. Start with one leg up in 75 degrees of hip flexion with the knee bent slightly less than 90 degrees and the foot in the dorsiflexed position. The down leg should be straight with the weight driving through the ball of the foot. Brace the core. On a coach's or partner's command, quickly punch the down leg to the up position and the up leg to the down position, then switch back. For each repetition, quickly return to the start position after switching the legs once each. Perform five repetitions. Rest for 60 seconds, then repeat, starting with the other leg up, for a total of two to four sets.

Wall Drill Three-Count

Equipment

Wall, partner

Procedure

Assume the setup position for the wall drill. Start with one leg up in 75 degrees of hip flexion with the knee bent slightly less than 90 degrees and the foot in the dorsiflexed position. The down leg should be straight with the weight driving through the ball of the foot. Brace the core. On a coach's or partner's command, quickly punch the down leg to the up position and the up leg to the down position, switch back, and then switch again to end in the start position but with the opposite leg up. For each repetition, switch the legs three times with as much speed as possible without losing postural position. Perform five repetitions, alternating the starting leg each time. Rest for 60 seconds between sets. Complete three sets.

Rapid Fire

Equipment

Wall

Procedure

Assume the setup position for the wall drill. Start with one leg up in 75 degrees of hip flexion with the knee bent slightly less than 90 degrees and the foot in the dorsiflexed position. The down leg should be straight with the weight driving through the ball of the foot. Brace the core. On a coach's or partner's command, quickly punch the legs up and down, switching legs as rapidly as possible without compromising mechanics or posture, for six to eight seconds. Repeat for one or two sets with 60 seconds of rest between sets.

BULLET-BELT EXERCISES

The bullet belt is a great piece of equipment to use when working on speed mechanics. It features a Velcro-type strap with a rip cord, but the rip cord is not used in these exercises. The bullet belt allows for further progression of the mechanics developed through the wall drills; specifically, the athlete must focus more on bracing the core and on being aware of the mechanics of each leg action.

Bullet-Belt Partner March

Equipment

Bullet belt, partner

Procedure

Attach the bullet belt around the waist. Lean forward with a coach or partner providing resistance through the belt (figure 7.2a). Once maximal lean angle is achieved (the position right before the waist bends), begin the punch–drive mechanics developed in the wall drills (figure 7.2b). Use a marching tempo to complete 10 yards (or meters), then rest for 45 seconds. Perform for three repetitions, then rest for 90 seconds. Repeat for two more sets.

Figure 7.2   Bullet-belt partner march.

Bullet-Belt Partner-Resisted Run

Equipment

Bullet belt, partner

Procedure

Once the athlete becomes more fluid in using the bullet belt and executing the punch–drive mechanics, it is time to start adding speed to the drill. To that end, a partner-resisted run provides the needed resistance to maintain an appropriate lean for good mechanics but also provides a slight overload.

Attach the bullet belt, then lean forward with a coach or partner providing resistance through the belt. Once maximal lean angle is reached (the position right before the waist bends), begin the punch–drive action, but this time make it a running effort. Continue the resisted run for 10 yards (or meters), then rest for 60 seconds. Perform three more repetitions to complete the set. Rest for two minutes, then begin the next set. Complete two or three sets.

Contrast Sprint

Equipment

Bullet belt, partner

Procedure

Overloading enables the athlete to recruit muscles in order to apply more force against the additional resistance. One way to exploit overloading is to do what is called a contrast set by performing one repetition with partner resistance and then one without resistance. The goal is for the resistance repetition to trick the body into recruiting more muscular help and then repeat the action without resistance in hopes that the body provides the same extra muscular support, thus yielding a faster sprint.

To perform the drill, attach the bullet belt. Lean forward with a coach or partner providing resistance through the belt. Once the maximal lean angle has been reached (the position right before the waist bends), begin the punch–drive action with a running effort. Perform the resisted run for five yards (or meters), then rest for 60 seconds. Next, perform a free run (without resistance) for 10 to 15 yards (or meters) and rest for another 60 seconds before starting the next resisted repetition. Perform two or three repetitions and complete three or four sets, but stop if you are too fatigued or notice a drop in speed quality (sheer speed and technical quality). Rest for two to three minutes between sets. The goal is to stimulate the muscles while avoiding fatigue.

REACTIVE SPRINTING

Now that the athlete has worked on good acceleration mechanics, it is time to incorporate a reactive component. Doing so is very important because sport performance requires unpredictable changes of speed.

Push-Up Sprint

Equipment

Partner

Procedure

Start in a prone position on the ground with the hands to the sides, as in the bottom position of a push-up (figure 7.3*a*). Stay relaxed and, on a coach's or partner's command, explode from the ground (figure 7.3*b*) and begin sprinting with punch–drive mechanics (figure 7.3*c*). Sprint for 10 to 20 yards (or meters). Perform three to five repetitions with a rest of 60 to 90 seconds between repetitions. Perform one or two sets; rest for two to three minutes before doing a second set.

Figure 7.3 Push-up sprint: (*a*) start position; (*b*) exploding from the ground; (*c*) sprint.

Supine Roll to Sprint

Equipment

Partner

Procedure

Lie supine with the knees bent and the feet flat on the ground (figure 7.4a). On a partner's or coach's command, quickly roll to a prone position (figure 7.4b), explode to your feet (figure 7.4c), and begin sprinting with good punch-and-drive mechanics. Sprint for 10 to 20 yards (or meters). Perform three to five repetitions with a rest of 60 to 90 seconds between repetitions. Perform one or two sets; rest for two to three minutes before doing a second set.

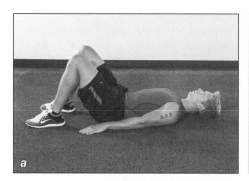 

Figure 7.4   Supine roll to sprint: (a) lie on back; (b) roll to prone position; (c) explode to feet.

Partner Sprint Chase

Equipment

Partner

Procedure

This drill provides a great way to incorporate competition into speed training. Use the start position for either the push-up sprint (figure 7.3) or the supine roll to sprint (figure 7.4). Both athletes assume the start position, but one acts as the leader and the other acts as the shadow (figure 7.5a). Once the leader initiates movement, the shadow does his or her best to catch the leader within the prescribed distance of the drill (figure 7.5b). The sprint distance is 10 to 20 yards (or meters). Complete three repetitions with a rest of 60 to 90 seconds between repetitions; alternating serving as leader and serving as shadow. Perform one or two sets with two to three minutes of rest between sets.

Figure 7.5   Partner sprint chase: (a) start position; (b) sprint.

AGILITY

Martial artists need to understand the difference between footwork training and agility training. Footwork-based exercises are used to develop pure quickness and foot coordination. Agility training, on the other hand, addresses how the athlete maneuvers around obstacles. Both footwork and agility drills help the athlete improve by developing skills such as balance, awareness, and reaction. This skill development can be done in a few different ways. As in every sport, footwork and movement skills are inherently specific to the skills of the chosen discipline; however, robust development of general skills allows the martial artist to increase his or her sport-specific ability. Simply stated, the better a martial artist develops his or her awareness and body control, the more well-rounded he or she can be.

FOOTWORK EXERCISES

Footwork is crucial to developing rhythm and timing, which is a must for all athletes who seek to master their craft. Temporal patterns can be established through simple drills, such as rope jumping, line hops, and agility ladders.

Footwork drills can also serve other purposes. For example, they may allow the athlete to identify side dominance or imbalance or to discover confidence (or lack thereof) in one leg or the other. These drills can also be used to rehabilitate after a lower limb injury, thus restoring coordination in the injured limb. Footwork drills elicit a fast neural response based on the speed of repetition, which can be increased once the drill is learned.

In and Out

Equipment

Partner

Procedure

Stand in an athletic position with the feet slightly narrower than the hips. On a partner's or coach's command, move your feet in and out (figure 7.6a and b) as fast as possible while maintaining the athletic position. The drill lasts 8 to 10 seconds, followed by 30 seconds of rest. Perform six to eight repetitions.

Figure 7.6   In and out: (a) feet in; (b) feet out.

Hip Rotation

Equipment

Agility ladder

Procedure

Stand in an athletic position with the feet hip-width apart. Keeping the shoulders square, rotate the feet and hips 45 degrees back and forth for 8 to 10 seconds (figure 7.7). Rest for 30 seconds. Perform three to six repetitions.

Figure 7.7   Hip rotation: (*a*) start position; (*b*) rotate hips to the left; (*c*) rotate hips to the right.

Line Hop

Equipment

Line on a court or field

Procedure

Stand with the feet spaced narrowly. Hop back and forth over a line as quickly as possible for 8 to 10 seconds (figure 7.8). Rest for 30 seconds. Perform three to six repetitions.

Figure 7.8 Line hop: (a) start position; (b) hop to the right over the line; (c) hop to the left over the line.

Medicine-Ball Toe Touch

Equipment

Medicine ball

Procedure

Stand with the knees slightly bent and a medicine ball at the feet. Hop on one foot and tap the medicine ball with the other foot (figure 7.9). Continue this pattern of alternating the feet while moving either clockwise or counterclockwise around the ball. As you become more proficient in the drill, alternate directions on a coach's or partner's command. Continue the drill for 8 to 10 seconds. Rest for 30 seconds. Perform three to six repetitions.

Figure 7.9 Medicine-ball toe touch.

AGILITY EXERCISES

Agility requires a blend of footwork and speed work. More generally, athletic development depends on putting the pieces together to best maneuver around an obstacle. Because martial arts require the practitioner to react, agility is a key piece in the overall development of a martial artist. Early in training, the drills presented here may take some time to learn, but once the necessary motor skills have been acquired, these drills can be made more reactive or used for additional conditioning.

Partner Reactive Shuffle

Equipment

Partner

Procedure

Stand in an athletic position facing the partner. One partner acts as the leader and the other as the shadow. The leader begins to shuffle from side to side at his or her discretion. The shadow follows the leader's pattern as closely as possible for the duration of the drill (figure 7.10*a* through *d*). Maintain a low athletic position with the feet wider than the hips to provide the best balance and ability to change direction. The drill lasts for 8 to 10 seconds, followed by a rest of 30 seconds. Perform three to six repetitions and switch roles with each repetition.

Figure 7.10   Partner reactive shuffle.

Box Drill

Equipment

Four cones

Procedure

Set up four cones in a box shape that measures 8 yards (or meters) per side (figure 7.11). Starting at one cone, sprint forward to the first cone, then quickly decelerate and transition into a side shuffle to the next cone. Decelerate, turn quickly, and sprint to the next cone. Decelerate and shuffle back to the starting cone. Rest for 30 seconds, then repeat. Complete four to six repetitions, alternating sides with each repetition.

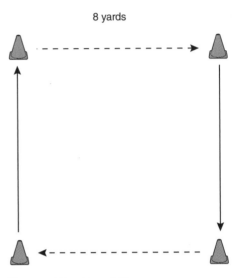

Figure 7.11   Box drill.

Lateral Hurdle Run

Equipment

Four cones or small hurdles

Procedure

Place four cones or small hurdles about 18 inches (45 cm) apart in a line. Standing lateral to (facing the line and standing at one end of it) the cones or hurdles, run down and back laterally with a knee-punch action for 10 seconds (figure 7.12). Rest for 30 seconds, then repeat. Complete four to six repetitions, alternating sides.

Figure 7.12   Lateral hurdle run.

Lateral Speed Shuffle

Equipment

Seven cones

Procedure

Place seven cones about two to three feet (0.6 to 0.9 m) apart in a line. Begin in a low athletic position. Quickly shuffle back and forth weaving around the cones while maintaining a good wide base with the feet (figure 7.13). Attack through the cones laterally while moving slightly forward until the athlete maneuvers through all the cones. Make sure to alternate the starting side on subsequent repetitions. Rest for 30 seconds. Perform four to six repetitions.

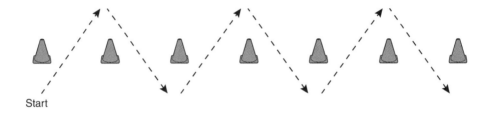

Figure 7.13 Lateral speed shuffle.

Figure 7.13 *(continued)*

CONCLUSION

This chapter presents just a few speed and agility drills from which the martial artist can choose. Remember that the goal is not to do a thousand different drills; instead, the goals are to develop one's agility, add speed, and exercise better body control. Ultimately, then, the key consideration is how this type of drill fits into the overall training plan. Be creative with the drills, but avoid falling into the trap of doing a drill simply for the sake of doing a drill. In addition, be sure that each drill is done in good athletic position, with equal weight distributions and a phenomenal sense of body control. Avoid speeding up a drill if doing so sacrifices technique. Understand that movement and resistance complement the end goal of optimizing human performance in martial arts.

Chapter 8

Recovery and Nutrition

In martial arts, there is often a fine line between winning and losing. It's easy to err on the side of more training and less recovery in hopes of garnering wins. Indeed, martial artists are typically motivated to immerse themselves in more work, which they justify with the thought of outworking the opponent. The truth, however, is that the best martial artist works *smarter* than the opponent—tactically—while being the best prepared physically.

A well-selected series of training steps—stimulation, accumulation, regeneration, and adaptation—produce the desired outcome. Regeneration, or recovery, doesn't happen automatically; it must be planned strategically and with precision to allow for the greatest adaptation to stress or workload.

The human body's involuntary functions are handled by the autonomic nervous system (ANS; figure 8.1), which is divided into the parasympathetic nervous system (PNS) and the sympathetic nervous system (SNS). The SNS controls the fight-or-flight response, and the PNS controls and restores homeostasis—the body's rest-and-digest response (table 8.1). Due to training intensity and the nature of martial arts, many martial artists spend much of their time in a sympathetic state, which can lead to decreased performance and promote overtraining. For this reason, it is imperative to incorporate recovery methods that do not distract the martial artist but rather allow her or him to fully dedicate the mind to the daily recovery process.

Information on nutrition and hydration was contributed by Rebeccah Sims.

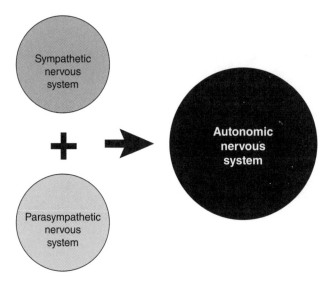

Figure 8.1 The sympathetic nervous system and parasympathetic nervous system combine to make up the autonomic nervous system.

Table 8.1 Comparison of Sympathetic and Parasympathetic Responses

Sympathetic response	Parasympathetic response
Increase in the rate and constriction of the heart	Decrease in heart rate
Dilation of bronchial tubes in the lungs and pupils in the eyes	Constriction of bronchial tubes in the lungs and pupils in the eye
Contraction of muscles	Relaxation of muscles
Release of adrenaline from the adrenal gland	N/A
Conversion of glycogen to glucose to provide fuel for the muscles	N/A

Not all recovery sessions are created equal. Some days may feature 10 minutes of an active, dynamic cool-down; other days may consist of breathing exercises or be dedicated solely to 45 to 60 minutes of low-intensity circuits (3-4 exercises done back to back); and still other days may include 30 minutes of self-myofascial release using various stretching tactics followed by low-level stability exercises. These methods are addressed in a later section of the chapter that also covers how they fit into a healthy training plan.

This chapter shows you how to use daily and weekly methods for maximizing training through smart recovery. The strategies covered in this chapter for nutrition, hydration, sleep, and regeneration help restore training homeostasis (figure 8.2) and allow the athlete to fully adapt to the stress of training.

To comprehend the value of sport nutrition, you must first understand that training is a stimulus used to promote adaptations in the body. Any exertion or exercise causes mild breakdown of muscle fibers and stresses the nerves that fire the muscles. As a response to this slight aggravation, the body—when in recovery—repairs muscle tissue and adapts by strengthening both the neural bonds and the muscle fibers, thus creating a more

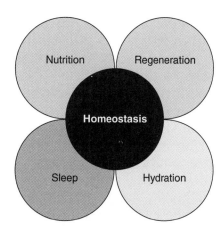

Figure 8.2 Homeostasis is restored when martial artists balance nutrition, hydration, sleep, and regeneration.

potent and efficient body than before. This process of regeneration is what creates the adaptations and advancements that lead to growth and athletic progression; training itself is planned only to stimulate this development. Therefore, recovery and repair of the body must be considered to be as important as the activity itself.

Optimal regeneration depends on proper nutrition. Without ideal and sufficient nutrients, the body lacks the necessary components for its development, thus making favorable growth and progression impossible. As a result, the athlete's training may be done in vain. Not only is nutrition critical for optimal performance and athletic progression, but also it plays a vital role in the martial artist's general health and well-being, which in turn may determine the outcome and length of his or her career.

FUNDAMENTALS OF GOOD NUTRITION

The human body is natural, and foods created by nature provide the finest sources of nutrition for the natural body. The body readily accepts these foods and uses them properly (as long as no allergies or sensitivities are present); therefore, they cause none of the negative effects seen with the intake of artificial and engineered substances and supplements. Everything ingested by the athlete interacts with the body's tissues, cells, and molecules; in the process, it either benefits or harms the body as a whole. Therefore, everything that the martial artist eats or drinks should contain only natural, pure, high-quality ingredients.

The human body is also governed by a primitive drive for survival. Even the well-trained athlete is wired with a highly sensitive protective mechanism. If the body detects any hint of insecurity or instability within its systems, it instantly reverts its focus and energy to functions that are necessary for maintaining life. Athletic growth and progress, of course, are not crucial to survival. However, when an athlete ensures stability, balance, and wellness through proper nutrition, he or she enables the body to invest more in the betterment of skill and athleticism. The athlete must always work with the body, not against it. When wellness and optimal functioning are prioritized, the athlete's body is able to tackle the challenges of athletic growth.

The martial artist faces a daily, ongoing responsibility to ensure that the body's basic needs are met. Doing so allows the body to function at its best and invest further in athletic development. The first key, and an indispensable one, is to maintain a standard of high-quality, natural food. Then, through the proper use of these nutrients, the athlete must establish stability within the body, so that it is secure and able to grow and progress.

Proper Hydration

Adequate hydration is the most important factor in creating stability in the body. Sufficient water must be present for the body to maintain its natural processes and support athletic growth. To meet this need, we must understand hydration as a constantly changing state that must be continuously monitored. Hydration level and volume of water loss are unique to each individual, and they vary greatly on the basis of multiple factors, including gender, size, body composition, temperature, humidity, altitude, and the activity performed. Therefore, instead of following general recommendations, the athlete must monitor hydration at all times.

Adequate hydration can be evaluated easily by monitoring the regularity of urination and the characteristics of the urine. A healthy athlete should urinate every few hours, and the urine should be odorless and clear to pale yellow. For those who participate in training sessions of very high intensity or long duration—as well as those in intense climates or extreme conditions—water loss should be closely monitored during both training and competition by tracking the disparity in body weight at the start and at the end of the activity. Every pound (0.5 kilogram) of water loss should be replenished with at least 16 ounces (0.5 liter) of water.

Healthy Eating

Along with proper hydration, athletic development also depends on sufficient and appropriate provision of all necessary nutrients. A good variety of high-quality, natural food provides the macronutrients and micronutrients needed to maintain physical health and advance athletic performance. Every meal must include plenty of high-quality macronutrients: carbohydrate, protein, and fat. Each macronutrient provides for the body in a unique way and is critical for health and optimal functioning. Depletion of a macronutrient—as seen, for example, in a low-carbohydrate diet—can be extremely detrimental to a martial artist's health and development.

In addition, it is best to vary the source of each macronutrient. For example, although free-range eggs are one of the most bioavailable (usable) sources of protein, an athlete should not eat only eggs but should include other sources of protein as well. By varying macronutrient sources, the martial artist not only combats digestive problems (e.g., food intolerance) but also helps prevent both depletion and excess accumulation of micronutrients. Eating a large variety of unaltered, plant-based foods (e.g., fruits, vegetables, and seeds) provides high-quality micronutrients and other beneficial substances.

Finally, the martial artist should eat regularly. Establish a pattern of eating that fits the daily schedule and stick to it as closely as possible. Providing the body with regular nutrients keeps it from regressing to a survival state; or to put it more positively, a set eating pattern helps the body prepare for training and competition.

SPECIFIC NUTRITION

Nutrition must be planned and properly timed, especially in relation to training sessions and competitions. Particular nutrients must be made available to the body at specific times in order to allow proper recovery and positive adaptations.

Before Training

Providing the body with adequate nutrition before a training session helps the athlete achieve prime execution in that session; it also prepares the athlete for proper recovery. Indeed, a small, powerful boost of helpful nutrients can make a considerable difference both in how the body trains and in its subsequent response. This is not the time for a big meal but for a small addition to what is consumed throughout the day. Most of all, the athlete should hydrate well, because the body needs a large amount of water to sustain the extra chemical reactions that occur during activity. Optimally, the athlete should eat or drink an hour and a half or two hours before the activity and then consume a couple cups of water 15 to 30 minutes before training begins.

Make sure that the snack or drink is not aggravating and can be digested easily and quickly. Good choices include low-glycemic carbohydrate sources and, if the activity will last more than two and a half hours, perhaps a small amount of easily digested protein. In addition, athletes who are training at lower intensities for long periods may benefit from ingesting a small amount of coconut, which is uniquely composed of faster-digesting fat.

Optimal carbohydrate options are sprouted whole grains and sprouted grain cereals or breads; certain fruits, such as apples, pears, peaches, and mangoes; activated barley; and small amounts of root vegetables, such as beets, carrots, and yucca. Good protein options are lean meat (e.g., fish, chicken breast); sprouted brown rice protein; and raw, organic, grass-fed whey protein concentrate.

In contrast, substances that are *not* easy to break down cause the body to direct energy and blood flow to the digestive system and away from the neuromuscular system. During training, this scenario may cause problems such as stomach issues; muscle stiffening; and sudden, inexplicable fatigue. For this reason, fat-dense items (e.g., most nuts and high-fat dairy products, including cheese) are not beneficial before exercise. Other items to avoid before training include most dairy (even low-fat), beef and other red meats, pork, high-protein foods, high-fiber foods, legumes (beans, peas, and peanuts), and cruciferous vegetables (e.g., cabbage, cauliflower, broccoli, Brussels sprouts, collards, and turnips).

After Training

The period after training is arguably the most crucial time in terms of sport nutrition. The body's response to training can be affected directly both by the timing of consumption and by the type of food ingested. Indeed, that food may determine the outcome of the workout—that is, whether it produces growth and adaptation or degeneration and possibly overtraining. After exertion, the body must be provided quickly with sufficient and appropriate nutrients in order to recover, rebuild, and progress from training. It is also critical to restore hydration.

After training, the body is very responsive to appropriate nutrients. The body is most receptive to nutrients during the first 15 minutes after training, and the next 45 minutes mark the final limit for optimal nutrient uptake. If given the right nutrients in either of these time frames, the body directly applies the nutrients to neuromuscular repair, which leads to optimal growth and adaptation. However, if these time periods pass without proper nutrition, the body focuses again on conserving energy instead of on growing. It may even start degenerating in an attempt to produce enough energy to tend to its fatigued self.

After a training session, rehydrate by drinking at least 10 ounces (0.3 liter) of water for each 30 minutes of training. If tracking weight loss during intense training, the athlete must replenish each pound

(0.5 kg) lost with at least 16 ounces (half a liter) of water. Since water loss varies by the individual, it is helpful to track hydration in order to ensure that it is ideal. Also continue to drink more water over the next few hours, because the body requires more water as it repairs itself from the training session. Pure coconut water, preferably organic and raw, is extremely beneficial and effective in replenishing water, electrolytes, and nutrient loss.

In nutritional terms, the ideal components for replenishment are fast-digesting and high-glycemic carbohydrate and fast-digesting protein. Indeed, in the hour after training, it is crucial to avoid fat of any kind; this is a unique instance in which fat is not beneficial, because it delays nutrient absorption and digestion. (This quality of fat is beneficial in other circumstances, such as nutrition for nighttime recovery or big meals.) Instead, in order to speed up digestion and absorption, nutrients may be supplied in liquid form. Some of the best options are raw whole fruit and fruit juices with raw, organic, grass-fed whey protein and raw honey.

Competition

Nutrition during competition should be similar to nutrition during training, not only because the demands on the body are similar, but also because a constant eating plan helps prepare the body optimally for competition. In the same way that a martial artist may benefit by performing the same daily warm-up in training, it can be useful to match competition nutrition to training nutrition. A regular eating plan may calm the martial artist, support optimal digestion, and even act as an internal warm-up, signaling the body that it will soon be time to perform.

Furthermore, everything ingested during competition should be familiar because the individual's reaction to a new item can never be guaranteed. This is not the time to try unfamiliar ingredients—even something known to be highly beneficial. Experiment with new foods at other times, such as the off-season and during small informal practices. Then, after ensuring a food's effectiveness and growing accustomed to it, the athlete can incorporate it into the competition plan.

The main goal of nourishment before competition is to provide powerful nutrients that allow the body to perform at its best without loading it down with the process of digestion. Therefore, nutrients ingested before competition must be easy to digest and provide steady and constant sustenance to the body. As in training, athletes in competition should ingest carbohydrate that is easy to digest, slow burning, and low glycemic. In this instance, it is also best if the carbohydrate is low in fiber, which can weigh down the digestive system. The plan may, however, include small quantities of highly digestible protein and fat. If nutrients are consumed close to competition time, consider providing them in liquid form (e.g., a shake or smoothie), which is more easily absorbed and boosts fluid intake.

Some martial arts events of high intensity and duration may also require nutrient replenishment during competition. A martial artist participating in an intense competition that lasts two and a half hours or more usually benefits from supplemental nutrients. Additional nourishment may also be needed during other competitions (e.g., tournaments) that consist of a number of shorter, high-intensity bouts. However, a break longer than three hours may be viewed as another precompetition time, and a bit more sustenance may therefore be consumed.

Nutrients ingested during competition should be instantly absorbable to replenish essential components such as water, electrolytes, and sometimes carbohydrate. Beyond hydration, which must be the primary focus, the body may also benefit from higher-glycemic carbohydrates, specifically those high in fructose, which are quickly and easily absorbed. A small quantity of protein is acceptable, but fat intake should be minimal. Food of any kind must be taken in small quantities with plenty of water. And again, all items should be familiar and proven to positively influence the individual during intense physical and mental pressure and exertion.

The martial artist must also consume adequate nutrients immediately after competition to aid in swift and effective recovery. This means proper supplementation in the minutes following competition and a highly nutritious meal soon afterward. Never should a martial artist lower his or her standards of high-quality nutrition after a competition. Instead, the athlete must focus on properly replenishing the body and allowing it to heal and progress from the competition in order to build and invest in future endeavors. Do not neglect the body after a competition by eating or drinking things that are unwholesome or unprofitable. It makes more sense to reward the body's efforts and accomplishments by allowing it to heal and progress.

SLEEP

Consistent and optimal sleep is one of the most overlooked aspects of training among all athletes, especially those in high school and college. Sleep provides the body's best opportunity to recover from the stress of the day. During various stages of sleep, the secretion of hormones (e.g., testosterone and growth hormone) helps regulate the stress hormone known as cortisol. Sleep cycles that are less than optimal create a sleep debt, which may have greater implications that lead to overtraining as the athlete's body is in rebuilding mode during sleep. Without adequate rest, the athlete may be working hard during the day but losing potential gains during the night.

Sleep needs are individual; there is no magic number of hours for feeling rested, and some athletes need more sleep than others do. The goal for each athlete, then, is to discover his or her own optimal amount of rest. For some athletes, seven hours is ideal, but others need nine hours or more to feel fully rested.

Sleep is also affected by many environmental factors—for example, work, deadlines, sickness, life stresses, and electronic devices in the bedroom—and it can be quite easy to fall into a sleep debt. The only way out of a sleep debt is to become aware of it. Another possible disruption is sleep apnea (a potentially serious problem when an individual stops breathing as they sleep). This can lead not only to disturbed sleeping patterns, but death in extreme cases; if this problem is suspected, consult a physician. In addition, some people simply have a tendency to be night owls.

Whatever the cause, a lack of deep sleep can put an athlete behind in the recovery process. To improve sleep, try the following strategies.

- Establish a consistent sleep and wake schedule, including weekends. If eight hours is the best sleep duration, get that eight hours not between midnight and 8 a.m. but from 10 p.m. to 6 a.m. Good sleep depends on more than the number of hours; it also matters *when* the hours occur. Many athletes reading this book may have a full-time job, family, or other commitments and scheduling an earlier bedtime can allow the athlete a better chance of having a full night's rest.

- Create a regular, relaxing bedtime routine—for example, listening to soothing music, reading nonstimulating books, or journal writing about the just-completed day's (or the next day's) training.

- Implement a routine of mindful, deep breathing before bed.

- Create a conducive sleeping environment—no television, computer, or mobile phone in the bedroom!

- Avoid caffeine in the evening and finish eating two to three hours before bedtime.

- Avoid watching the news or other stimulating content before bedtime.

REGENERATION METHODS

Nutrition, hydration, and sleep are all important, but recovery can also be aided by other methods that decrease the needed recovery time between sessions. Regeneration strategies can be as simple as cooling down after a training session; alternatively, they can involve specialized massage and other therapies. The decision about which methods to use is usually driven by cost and time. The good news is that you don't need full access to a training room to reap the benefits; less expensive alternatives can also help accelerate the healing process.

Self-Myofascial Release (Foam Roll)

Lie on a foam roller and target large muscle groups by rolling the length of the muscle—for example, from the hip down to the knee. When rolling across the foam roller, body weight contributes to the self-massage. Usually, 20 to 30 seconds per muscle group will suffice. Initially, the athlete may experience a high pain response, but it will lessen if the work is done consistently. The best muscles to target with the needed leverage into the roller are the quadriceps, hamstring, lateral thigh, gluteus maximus, erector spinae, pectoralis major, and latissimus dorsi (figure 8.3a through e). Due to the potential pain response, it is best to use the foam roller only after a workout or on recovery days. Never use it before ballistic activity because the pain response that is produced from the release may evoke a relaxation signal to the muscles and decrease stiffness. This inhibition response may not be ideal for high power output and joint stability.

Figure 8.3   Foam roller exercises: (a) IT band; (b) quad.

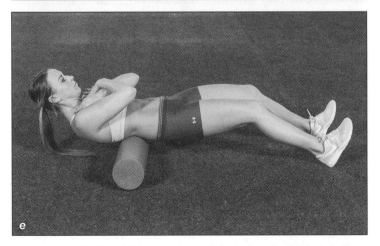

Figure 8.3   Foam roller exercises: (*c*) piriformis; (*d*) hamstring; (*e*) erector spinae.

Cold Bath or Ice Bath

Why take a cold bath or ice bath? The cold water induces vasoconstriction or a narrowing of the blood vessels. Then, when you complete the bath and your core temperature rises, you experience a rush of blood to the extremities that helps eliminate toxins and delivers nutrients to the tissues while helping to decrease inflammation. The desired temperature range for a cold bath is 60 to 75 degrees Fahrenheit (16 to 24 degrees Celsius), whereas the target for an ice bath is about 55 degrees Fahrenheit (13 degrees Celsius). You can either stand or sit in the bath. Limit the time to five to eight minutes in an ice bath and no more than 10 minutes in a cold bath.

Contrast Bath

Use two tubs—one cold (55 to 59 degrees Fahrenheit, or 13 to 15 degrees Celsius) and one hot (98 to 102 degrees F, or 37 to 39 degrees C). Alternate between the baths for one minute in the cold bath followed immediately by two minutes in the hot bath. Continue this cycle for three rounds. The cold creates vasoconstriction, and the hot produces vasodilation. When alternated, the process creates a vascular pump that helps flush toxins and transport nutrients to the tissues to aid the recovery process.

Recovery Breathing

Lie on your back with the knees bent. Take a deep nasal breath, inhaling as deeply as you can. Slowly exhale through the mouth with the lips open only slightly to slow the rate of exhalation. The exhalation should be twice as long as the inhalation and become forceful at the end as you use your abdominal muscles to exhale fully. Repeat for 10 breaths, then lie motionless for 10 minutes while relaxing as much as possible. Recovery breathing is a great way to seamlessly transition highly intensive efforts of the training session (sympathetic) into the recovery process (parasympathetic) of the training session.

Active Isolated Stretching (AIS)

AIS involves a series of dynamic stretches using a band that include a contraction from the opposite muscle group in order to relax the muscles targeted by the stretch (figure 8.4a through d). For example, when stretching the hamstrings, the initial contraction comes from the quadriceps and the hip flexors, which sends a message to the hamstrings to relax in order to move the muscle in a greater range of motion. Remember that stretching isn't always about how far you go into a specific range of motion itself, but about how well you control the speed and tempo within the range (referring back to the stability of the range). Many attempt to stretch a muscle as far as possible without a real concern of what other ranges of motion they may be violating. It is not uncommon to focus solely on a stretch and put great strain or stress on connective tissues.

Figure 8.4   Active isolated stretches: (*a*) leg raise; (*b*) abduction; (*c*) adduction; (*d*) leg cradle.

Barefoot Cool-Down

Use the exercises from the quadruped series, straight-leg series, hip rotation series, and dynamic flexibility series presented in chapter 3. Perform the exercises while barefoot. Hold the positions for three to five seconds to ensure that the balance is secure and stable. Many athletes will cool down after a workout on a stationary bike, treadmill, or elliptical. Using the barefoot cool-down will not only help flush the post-workout toxins, but can also serve as a great tool to reinforce balance and posture after a strenuous session.

Active Recovery Sequence (ARS)

The ARS sequence blends foam-roller myofascial release, AIS, and the barefoot cool-down to create a 20- to 30-minute session. The rationale is simple: Decrease muscular tightness with the foam roller, then use active isolated stretches to take the relaxed muscle groups through a greater range of motion, and finally use the barefoot series to solidify the new ranges of motion.

During the AIS part of the sequence, take care not to force the end range of motion. Use slow, deliberate motions and return to the start position without subjecting the tissue to any stress or trauma.

The barefoot exercises add a stability component to the new range of motion. Following the myofascial exercises and the AIS with the barefoot cool-down exercises helps ensure stability and muscular integrity at end ranges of motion.

MAT, ART, Massage, and Dry Needling

MAT (muscle activation techniques), ART (active release therapy), massage, and dry needling (when a needle is inserted into a tight or restricted muscle tissue in order to send a spasm or contraction to the muscle, which in turn sends an inhibitory signal to relax) are specialized therapies that must be performed by a licensed or certified therapist. These techniques attempt to increase muscular efficiency and decrease muscle tightness through touch or specific trigger points that elicit a contract–relax response. Daily self-myofascial massage, barefoot cool-downs, cold and ice baths, and recovery breathing help promote the parasympathetic response so that the martial artist can maneuver out of the fight-or-flight response of the sympathetic nervous system that they constantly encounter.

CONCLUSION

Though training is important for the martial artist, recovery is equally important, if not more so, but techniques used can depend on time and budget. In order to ensure that training leads to gain rather than loss, the athlete must practice and implement good sleep hygiene, effective hydration strategies, and a well-balanced and optimally timed nutrition plan. Remember that adaptation occurs only if the athlete recovers properly from training sessions. In contrast, dehydration, malnourishment, and sleep debt cause more stress to the body, delay adaptation, and perhaps lead to overtraining. With these realities in mind, the martial artist's goal should not be to outwork the opponent but to train optimally, both tactically and physically, in order to beat the opponent.

Chapter 9

Program Planning and Periodization for Martial Arts

Effective organization of the martial artist's training schedule is critical for success. Athletes often believe that simply completing a practice week ensures success in learning new skills or adapting to better fitness levels and performance abilities. However, completing a practice week does not benefit the athlete if the quality of training is compromised or if strength and conditioning are not optimally aligned with tactical training.

The goal of this chapter is to give you the tools to organize training in a way that maximizes gains. When training is approached systematically and with accountability, the martial artist can maximize his or her efforts and showcase the hard work and sacrifices made in order to master the craft.

UNDERSTANDING PERIODIZATION

Periodization is a strategy used to help athletes develop specific, long-term, athletic qualities; prevent overtraining; and taper and peak for specific events. The key to periodization is to effectively manipulate training variables such as intensity, volume, and exercise selection. Simply stated, periodization helps athletes maximize recovery in order to elicit better performance. However, when it comes to peaking for an event or making a training plan, no two situations or athletes are the same. A training plan that works for one athlete may not work for another. Therefore, the training plan must be developed for the individual athlete.

A well-designed periodization plan provides a great tool, but to develop it we need to answer certain questions. What is the athlete's training status—novice, intermediate, or advanced? What is the athlete's chronological age (meaning actual age), biological age (looking specifically at adolescent athletes who may all be the same age yet others have physically/biologically matured faster), and training age (meaning how many years of quality training does the athlete currently have tactically and strength conditioning-wise)? What is the time frame for reaching specific goals? Is this time frame realistic and optimal for a successful outcome?

Periodization can be confusing, and the use of terms and definitions from different languages and translations can make it difficult for practitioners to agree or effectively implement a program. The goal here, then, is not to get caught up in terminology but to understand the underlying strategy.

Training must be geared to specific objectives in order to elicit a positive response. Training serves as the stressor or stimulus, which is followed by an accumulated workload over a given time, which in turn is followed by restoration or a deloading week to allow the body to catch up or recover from the work done (figure 9.1). Once the restoration phase has occurred, the athlete has adapted to the stimulus, which results in increased ability. Training can focus on endurance, strength, power, speed, or, to some degree, all of these qualities depending on the chosen training model, the goal of the training block (theme), and the athlete's development level.

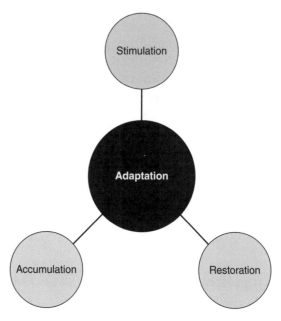

Figure 9.1 Stimulation, accumulation, and restoration all lead to adaptation.

Table 9.1 shows the building blocks of a long-term plan. A quadrennial cycle typically centers on long-term planning for athletes who compete at the international level; however, coaches can also use it with athletes with whom they will work for multiple years, as in high school or college sports. This level of planning should be viewed as a sort of blueprint that is helpful in setting a plan and showing direction. Of course, many things can change in the course of four years, but a quadrennial cycle sets a plan and a goal to structure the work of training.

Table 9.1 Periodization Cycle Hierarchy

Periodization cycle	Description
Quadrennial cycle	Plan covering 4 years or more
Macrocycle	Typically 1 year
Mesocycle	Typically 3 or 4 weeks; unit that makes up a macrocycle
Microcycle	Typically 1 week; unit that makes up a mesocycle
Workout	Structural unit that makes up a microcycle

The next level down in terms of specificity is the macrocycle, which covers a calendar year of training and competition. For the macrocycle, the coach narrows the lens a bit in order to decide which competitions to prioritize for tapering and peaking. Most events require a taper, but the athlete should highlight the most important events for her or his level of competence.

This one-year plan still needs to allow some wiggle room, but not as much as is needed for the quadrennial cycle. Still, during this year of preparation, the athlete has time to focus on and eradicate physical and technical weaknesses. Another way to view both the quadrennial cycle and the macrocycle is to liken them to a syllabus that lays out goals and objectives for students to meet during a yearlong course.

The next level of specificity is the mesocycle, which serves as the building block for the macrocycle. A mesocycle can be as short as two weeks or as long as six weeks, but most mesocycles last four weeks. At this point, the lens of planning narrows even more as we aim at the training target. A mesocycle typically includes three weeks of progressive workload (stimulation and accumulation) and one week of restitution or deloading (adaptation).

Whatever the goal (e.g., endurance, strength, power, or speed) of a given block of training, that goal should be the focal point of the majority of the exercises, as well as the set and repetition scheme. If engaged in a strength block, for example, it would not make sense to use a set-and-repetition scheme geared to endurance. Make sure that the process matches the goal.

At the same time, at the mesocycle level of programming, the coach can start customizing the training program based on how well the athlete is—or is not—recovering from the stress of training. In other words, the mesocycle can include some wiggle room in terms of total workloads and intensities, as well as work-around variables (such as the inevitable vagaries of life!).

This caveat calls to mind a term coined in the book *Super Training* by Mel Siff—"cybernetic periodization"—which refers to the strategy of using a combined objective and subjective system. In this approach, the athlete still follows a periodized template but has wiggle room to make adjustments based on overall feel. For example, the athlete can pull back on some days and really go after it on other days, depending on how he or she feels. This type of adjustment can be made on the basis of a simple concept referred to as the rating of perceived exertion (RPE), in which the athlete evaluates how each workout or priority lift feels on a scale of 1 to 10. This system gives the athlete the autonomy to make the best decisions in light of the upcoming practice schedule and how well he or she is recovering from the stress of training.

The building block of the mesocycle is the microcycle, which can range from one day (or workout) to a full training week. The microcycle is typically the planning unit that is most subject to adjustment based on subjective analysis by the coach or athlete. We are now focused on the immediate target. At the same time, we still hold the larger view in mind to keep us mindful of the desired outcome of the individual training sessions or weeks that make up the mesocycle. To return to an earlier analogy, if the quadrennial cycle and macrocycle can be viewed as a course syllabus, the microcycle can be viewed as a teacher's daily lesson plan that helps build the foundation for achieving the overall course goal.

Table 9.2 provides a quick reference guide to the variables addressed in a periodization plan: volume, intensity, RPE (cybernetic periodization), and exercise selection. Volume is defined as the total number of sets and repetitions; distance is also considered in training geared toward speed, agility, and conditioning.

Intensity is the percentage of maximal effort used. In the weightroom, intensity is measured as a percentage of a 1-repetition maximum (1RM) in the priority lifts. For other exercises, intensity is expressed in terms of watts (power) or, for sprinting and sparring, perceived effort, which is of course a relatively subjective measure in keeping with the concept of cybernetic periodization.

Finally, exercise selection shifts from general to specific as the calendar year passes. Early in training, exercise choices can be very general and nonspecific in order to build a foundation. Over time, as the mesocycles become more specific to the chosen sporting goals, exercise selections should shift to multijoint, multiplanar, and faster forms of movement.

Table 9.2 Periodization Loading Parameters

Volume	Sets, reps, distance, and how many total exercises
Intensity	Effort described in terms % 1RM, watts, % of max heart rate, or (in sprinting or sparring) perceived effort in
RPE (cybernetic periodization)	Subjective sense of the effect of each lift or session on the individual
Exercise selection	Shift from general to specific over time

MODELS OF PERIODIZATION

Chapter 2 provided evaluation protocols for establishing a baseline understanding of a martial artist's strengths and weakness. Using this data, you can make the best decisions about utilizing the training model in a truly individual manner. Other chapters cover exercises that address a range of needs, such as warming up, explosive power, and speed. We must view all such exercises, as well as training strategies, as ingredients to be used in the recipe of programming and periodization. If we add the right ingredients at the right time and in the right sequence, we produce the best outcome.

The most common model is linear, or traditional, periodization. Linear periodization plans can produce great results for novice and intermediate athletes. However, athletes who possess a more extensive training background may benefit from more advanced models, such as undulated periodization, because their training requires more variation in order to elicit a stimulus response. Undulated periodization offers a good in-season model for maintaining performance; it can also serve as a highly effective tool for advanced athletes whose competition cycle lacks sufficient time to follow the linear model.

Remember that microcycles make up mesocycles and that mesocycles make up macrocycles. Whatever the theme for a given mesocycle, the microcycles should match it. For example, if the mesocycle theme is power, it would be counterproductive at the microcycle level to use a set-and-repetition scheme that mimics endurance. Referring back to the SAID principle—specific adaptation to imposed demand (chapter 1)—the body adapts to what it is trained for.

Each phase of training builds on the preceding phase (figure 9.2). For example, an athlete must develop a broad foundation of muscular endurance in order to better express strength. The better the athlete's strength, the better opportunity he or she has to generate power. In turn, the more power the athlete has, the more likely she or he is to produce speed. This progressive process is referred to as phase potentiation. Simply stated, it means that all previously developed qualities help underpin the next stage or phase of training.

A typical macrocycle is divided into four main parts: general physical preparation (GPP), specific physical preparation (SPP), competition, and peaking and maintenance (table 9.3). In the GPP phase, the typical goal is to increase work capacity or base conditioning while blending in strength

Figure 9.2   Phase potentiation means that each phase of training builds on the foundation laid by the preceding phase.

Table 9.3   Four Phases of a Macrocycle

	General physical preparation (GPP)	Specific physical preparation (SPP)	Competition	Peaking and maintenance
Objective	Strength, endurance	Strength, power	Strength, power, speed	Specific speed, active rest
Load	Low to moderate	High	High	Very high to low
Volume	High	Moderate to high	Low	Very low
Repetitions	8–20	3–6	2 or 3	1–3
Sets	3–5	3–5	3–5	1–3
Days per week	3	3	2 or 3	1

work. The SPP phase includes more strength and power development. The competition involves blending strength, power, and speed. Peaking involves maintaining these qualities with a priority on sport-specific speed—for example, the speed of strikes, kicks, throws, and takedowns.

Table 9.3 provides a quick guide to help the athlete make the best choices based on long-term and short-term training goals. For example, if testing reveals that an athlete is deficient in speed, her or his natural inclination might be to work exclusively on exercises for speed and power. This rationale is not completely wrong—nor is it completely right. Even test results showing low speed and power do not mean that an athlete's training should go in only one direction. Remember that all qualities help lay the foundation for the next phase.

BUILDING AN INDIVIDUAL PLAN

Having developed an understanding of the building blocks that make up periodization, it is now time to take a realistic look at the life of a martial artist. How many practices are done per week? How many technical and intensive bouts? What is the duration of each practice? These questions must be answered before one begins to implement a strength and conditioning program. Realistically, most martial artists need only two or three days per week of strength and conditioning; this frequency both fits their schedules and prevents overtraining. In addition, many conditioning strategies can be implemented at the end of a tactical session in order to help minimize the total number of training sessions per week (tables 9.4 and 9.5).

Tables 9.4 and 9.5 present generic schedules for martial artists; that is, they simply show how to organize and best qualify total training volume. Once a schedule has been put in place, the athlete should identify the rating of perceived exertion (RPE) either by using a scale of 1 to

Table 9.4   Novice (Noncompetitor)

	Tactical	Strength	Conditioning
Monday	×		×
Tuesday		×	
Wednesday	×		×
Thursday		×	
Friday	×		×
Saturday		×	
Sunday	Off		

Table 9.5   Intermediate or Advanced (Competitor)

	Tactical	Technical	Strength	Conditioning
Monday		×	×	
Tuesday	×			×
Wednesday		×	×	
Thursday	×			×
Friday		×	×	
Saturday	×			×
Sunday	Off			

10 (1 for easy and 10 for hard) or by assigning one of three colors to the training session (red for hard, yellow for moderate, or green for easy). This approach not only helps determine how hard each practice is, but also aids in evaluation of accumulated fatigue. For example, a practice that is usually rated yellow but gets rated red on a given day makes you aware of accumulated fatigue, thus enabling you to manage it.

It is critical for the martial artist to map out training needs. Regardless of the tactical theme of the day, the majority of conditioning comes from tactical sessions that use either a live tempo (which resembles a sparring pace) or a technical tempo (which is lower in intensity and has a more rhythmic flow). General conditioning can be done to further enhance the aerobic pathway or raise the lactate threshold post practice; however, too much conditioning could produce overkill and detract from the martial artist's ability to be explosive or use effective speed in combat. Good planning requires give and take during periods of concurrent (training multiple abilities at the same time) training in order to simultaneously develop the biomotor abilities that make up athleticism. This organization of training helps you make better choices when structuring the strength and conditioning program based on what the athlete isn't getting in their training week.

LINEAR PERIODIZATION

Linear periodization, also known as the traditional model, is the most common approach and is best suited to novice and intermediate athletes—classifications that refer to training age, referring to strength and conditioning and not how long or how exceptional an athlete is in the chosen discipline. For athletes with a young training age, training does not need to involve a tremendous amount of variation; to the contrary, the mere addition of a structured resistance plan allows most of these athletes to become stronger and more explosive. However, as an athlete advances in training age, and the training stressor loses its novelty, more variation is needed to help the athlete retain and build on the developed physical qualities.

Linear periodization can best be described as wave periodization. Typically, a mesocycle includes three weeks of gradually increasing intensity and one week of deloading that is used as active recovery. If this scheme is repeated, a graphic representation of it looks like a series of waves. For example, figure 9.3 presents a generic graph showing a consistent rise in intensity over three weeks followed by a deloading fourth week.

In the following examples of the linear (traditional) model, the indicated ratios (e.g., 3:1, 4:1) simply represent the number of loaded and unloaded weeks. Adding a fourth week of loading is one way to increase training volume as the athlete begins to adapt to the training stress. Some of the examples also indicate a decrease in load in addition to the deload week itself, but the athlete should maintain a high level of execution speed even during these times, especially during the deloading week in blocks focused on strength, power, or speed.

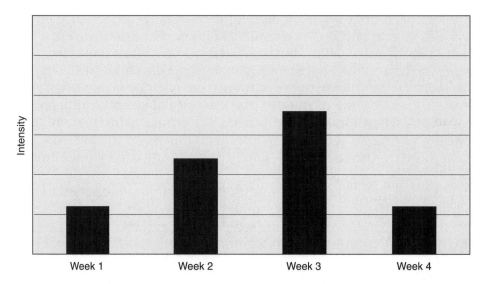

Figure 9.3 Fluctuation of intensity over a four-week mesocycle with three loaded weeks and one deloaded week.

Linear Example: Muscular Endurance (4:1)

Week 1: 1 set of 12 to 15 repetitions per exercise

Week 2: 2 sets of 12 to 15 repetitions per exercise

Week 3: 3 sets of 12 to 15 repetitions per exercise

Week 4: 4 sets of 12 to 15 repetitions per exercise

Week 5: 1 set of 12 to 15 repetitions per exercise (deloading)

Linear Example: Strength (3:1)

Week 1: 2 sets of 6 to 8 repetitions per exercise

Week 2: 3 sets of 6 to 8 repetitions per exercise

Week 3: 3 or 4 sets of 6 repetitions per exercise

Week 4: 2 sets of 6 repetitions per exercise (deloading)

Linear Example: Strength and Power (3:1)

Week 1: 3 sets of 4 to 6 repetitions per exercise

Week 2: 5 sets of 4 to 6 repetitions per exercise

Week 3: 5 sets of 3 to 5 repetitions per exercise

Week 4: 2 sets of 3 to 5 repetitions per exercise (deloading)

Linear Example: Power and Speed Based on 1 Rep Max \ 1RM (4:1)

Week 1: 3 sets of 3 to 5 repetitions per exercise (65 percent to 70 percent)

Week 2: 3 to 5 sets of 3 to 5 repetitions per exercise (70 percent to 75 percent)

Week 3: 5 sets of 3 repetitions per exercise (60 percent to 65 percent); load down, speed high

Week 4: 5 sets of 3 repetitions per exercise (50 percent to 55 percent); load down, speed high

Week 5: 3 sets of 1 to 3 repetitions per exercise (50 percent to 55 percent); load flat, speed high (deload)

Regardless of the theme of the mesocycle—muscular endurance, strength, strength and power, or power and speed—the strategy of the sets, repetitions, and loads remains relatively the same. This consistent strategy within the block of training allows one phase of training to set up the next.

UNDULATED PERIODIZATION

Undulated periodization can also be used to touch on all strength qualities in the same mesocycle. Sometimes, this strategy can be referred to as weekly undulating or summated mesocycles. This approach may be well suited to athletes who have an intermediate-level training history. Since these athletes have had significant exposure to strength and conditioning, they have established many of the strength qualities. In such cases, touching on all of the qualities in the same mesocycle provides a great way to raise or maintain all qualities, whereas focusing on a single quality for a full month might cause the other qualities to suffer. Imagine our strength qualities of endurance, strength, power, and speed as a performer spinning plates at the circus. As the performer has all plates (or strength qualities) spinning, but ignores one plate too long, the plate will begin to wobble, and if he doesn't provide enough attention to the plate it will fall. Now, imagine strength has been gained for our athlete and without enough attention to this quality, the athlete's strength may begin to suffer. However, if the quality is attended to like the plate, we can better preserve our athletes strength. This weekly undulated type of mesocycle might look something like the following example:

Weekly Undulating Periodization (2-3 workouts a week): Summated Mesocycle (4:1)

Week 1: 3 sets of 12 to 15 repetitions per exercise (muscular endurance)

Week 2: 3 or 4 sets of 6 to 8 repetitions per exercise (strength); 70 percent to 80 percent 1RM

Week 3: 4 or 5 sets of 3 to 5 repetitions per exercise (strength and power); 80 percent to 85 percent 1RM

Week 4: 5 sets of 3 to 5 repetitions per exercise (power and speed); 50 percent to 65 percent 1RM

Week 5: 3 sets of 1 to 3 repetitions per exercise (power and speed); 50 percent to 65 percent 1RM (deloading)

DAILY UNDULATION

The strategy of undulated periodization can be taken a step further through daily undulation. In this approach, one day is set aside during each week for each training quality. Daily undulation offers a good way for an athlete with sufficient training experience to touch on each quality during the week in order to best preserve endurance, strength, power, and speed. I find this model to be most beneficial in a training camp, where it allows the athlete to hold onto the performance qualities gained during the off-season while minimizing total fatigue as tactical training time increases.

Although the traditional periodization model works for many martial artists, the undulated model (table 9.6) provides a good training-camp strategy for a martial artist with an extensive background in resistance training. Most training camps for competition last 8 to 10 weeks. Given this time frame, undulated periodization provides a perfect way to

Table 9.6 Undulated Periodization Model (3:1)

	Monday	Wednesday	Friday
Week 1	Power and speed 3 sets 3–5 reps at 50%–55% IRM	Strength 3 sets 6–8 reps at 70%–75%	Muscular endurance 2 sets 12–15 reps at 60%
Week 2	Power and speed 3–5 sets 3–5 reps at 55%–65%	Strength 3 or 4 sets 6 reps at 75%–80%	Muscular endurance 3 sets 12–15 reps at 65%
Week 3	Power and speed 5 sets 3 reps at 65%–70%	Strength 4 sets 4–6 reps at 80%–85%	Muscular endurance 3 sets 12 reps at 70%
Week 4 (deloading)	Power and speed 1 or 2 sets 1–3 reps at 50%–55%	Strength 2 sets 6 reps at 70%	Muscular endurance 2 sets 12 reps at 60%

implement two mesocycles that consist either of three weeks loaded and one week unloaded (3:1) or four weeks loaded and one week unloaded (4:1). The last week in each case is treated as part of the taper for the training camp. The taper is discussed in more detail in chapter 12 as we use a step-down model to ensure optimal taper while also taking into consideration the possible need for a weight cut in combative sports that use specific weight classes.

During preparation for competition, the undulated periodization model allows the martial artist to maintain specific speed, power, strength, and endurance qualities. It also allows the athlete to make good decisions about strength and conditioning tactics while prioritizing sport training. In addition, the undulation of intensity and volume help the athlete manage the accumulative fatigue that sets in during a training camp for competition.

Remember, however, the undulated model is not the best choice if the athlete's training age or training exposure is insufficient. Such an athlete needs more foundational training to best stimulate all of the qualities of strength.

CONCLUSION

This chapter sets the stage for program design. Athletes and coaches can take a best-practices approach to designing a program when they ask the necessary questions about the athlete's developmental level, training age, chronological age, training schedule, competition schedule, and initial test results. The next two chapters delve into specific program designs for striking and kicking (chapter 10) and grappling and wrestling (chapter 11).

Chapter 10

Programs for the Striking and Kicking Arts

Having laid out the template for programming and periodization, it is now time to put together the master plan. As shown in chapter 9, the key to making the best road map for success is to develop a firm understanding of training demands throughout the week. More specifically, to develop the most effective striking and kicking, an athlete must lay a solid foundation of muscular endurance and strength, which ultimately leads to power and explosiveness. To succeed in combat, the athlete must be fast from the point of attack and wield enough power to repeatedly deliver ample force into the opponent. To achieve these goals, one must effectively handle multiple factors: exercise sequencing, selection, and execution; load selection; and determination of sets and repetitions.

The training plan must include all key elements of physical preparedness for biomotor abilities—speed, power, strength, agility, flexibility, coordination, and conditioning. These are the building blocks of performance success, and you must account for all of them during the training week. In addition to setting aside two or three days for strength and conditioning work, you can also integrate conditioning sessions at the conclusion of certain tactical sessions as needed. For example, an athlete who has a good aerobic foundation but poor lactate capacity and work capacity may benefit from doing one or two sets of post-session Tabata intervals (see sidebar for more on Tabata). This work serves as a great finisher, eliminates the need to perform an additional conditioning session on this day, and allows the athlete to save time by beginning the recovery process for the next day of training.

When setting up the week, address all training and recovery qualities in the best sequence to enhance the performance of each ability and to make best use of the available time for each session. The training sessions should not exceed 75 minutes from start to finish. The goal is to

WHAT IS TABATA TRAINING?

Tabata intervals, named after physician and researcher Izumi Tabata, have become extremely popular in the fitness and combat sport communities. Tabata is a type of high-intensity interval training that can produce great anaerobic and aerobic benefits. The work-to-rest ratio is two to one, which is usually executed in the pattern of a 20-second segment of work followed by a 10-second segment of rest; the pattern is typically performed for eight repetitions. The training can be done with no equipment other than body weight (as in burpees), with inexpensive equipment (e.g., jump rope), or with expensive equipment (e.g., VersaClimber).

Whichever particular exercise is selected, the athlete performs with high effort for 20 seconds, then rests for 10 seconds. Doing so becomes increasingly difficult as the set continues and therefore challenges the athlete's lactate threshold (as discussed in chapter 4). At the same time, based on the total exercise time, it also influences aerobic power. Thus, it addresses two crucial qualities for martial artists.

With anything good, however, there is often a potential downside. In this case, performing this type of interval without a substantial base of fitness results in poor execution and increased risk of injury; it may also cause the athlete to exceed his or her lactate threshold, which may lead to vomiting or passing out. With these pitfalls in mind, Tabata intervals should be approached not as an exciting exercise trend but as a strategy used sparingly after a good tactical session. They might also be used if an athlete has to sit out of tactical or sparring sessions due to injury or a skin infection (e.g., ringworm) that precludes having contact with other athletes.

integrate this training into the martial artist's schedule without compromising time and energy that needs to be spent on discipline-specific skill and tactical sessions.

BUILDING AN EFFECTIVE PROGRAM

Exercise selection and daily training theme are subject to the discretion of the practitioner. For the purposes of this book, there are always four categories of training: active dynamic warm-up; skill or movement emphasis for the day; resistance training (adjusted for the current block of training on the basis of endurance, strength, power, or speed); and recovery. To start building an individualized program, use the previous chapters as a reference guide and as a quick menu of options for exercise selection and modalities.

Depending on the martial artist's individual needs, you might make a trade-off between resistance training and more conditioning (or additional conditioning) after resistance training before recovery. In most cases, I would rather see traditional conditioning added at the end of a tactical session. In some instances, the aerobic capacity work can serve as a great active recovery after a live practice, or a lactate-capacity workout (e.g., Tabata) can provide a great way to finish a technical drilling session by pushing the lactate energy system. The bottom line is that the athlete has options and the autonomy to make the best decisions based on his or her needs.

Active Dynamic Warm-Up

To build the warm-up, pick three to five series each day. Table 10.1 lists some of the warm-up exercises. The warm-up can be nearly the same each day, which enables the athlete to rehearse it and master the movements, thus developing better range of motion and better control throughout the movement. Alternatively, the sequences can be varied as often as one likes. Either way, the goal is to get comfortable and prepare the body for the movement session that follows.

Table 10.1 Selected Warm-Ups

Monday	Wednesday	Friday
Quadruped series, p. 35	Squat series, p. 48	Shoulder series, p. 53
Straight-leg series, p. 41	Shoulder series, p. 53	Squat series, p. 48
Dynamic flexibility, p. 56	Dynamic flexibility, p. 56	Quadruped series, p. 35
Shoulder series, p. 53	Straight-leg series, p. 41	Dynamic flexibility, p. 56
Linear skip, p. 67	Carioca, p. 66	Linear skip or lateral A skip, p. 71

Movement

The movement emphasis can change from speed to agility each workout, or the session can feature blended days of both. The best part of these movement sessions is that they allow the martial artist to work in either the alactic or the lactic energy system depending on the duration and intensity of the drills. Pick three or four drills for each day and perform two or three repetitions with plenty of recovery time. The focus here is not on conditioning but on movement quality. Table 10.2 lists various drills and exercises.

Table 10.2   Selected Drills for Movement Emphasis

Monday	Wednesday	Friday
Backward A skip, p. 71	Tall side slide, p. 64	Line hop, p. 169
Wall drill (1, 2 and 3 count), pp. 158-160	Carioca, p. 66	Hip rotation, pp. 152, 168
Rapid fire (6 to 8 sec.), p. 160	Carioca knee punch, p. 67	Push-up sprint, pp. 150, 163
Bullet-belt partner march, p. 161	Supine roll to sprint, p. 164	Lateral speed shuffle, p. 174
Bullet-belt partner-resisted run, p. 162	Box drill, p. 172	Partner reactive shuffle, pp. 178, 171
10- and 20-yard sprints, p. 20	Spider drill, p. 23	Partner sprint chase, p. 165

Resistance

The specific emphasis of the resistance session can be adjusted in terms of repetitions and percent of effort on weight lifted. For example, if the goal is muscular endurance, you might use two or three sets of 12 to 15 repetitions or more in an intensity range of 60 to 70 percent effort based on 1-repetition max (1RM). If the goal is strength, you might use three to five sets of 1 to 5 repetitions in an intensity range of 80 to 100 percent effort based on 1RM values. And if the goal is power development, you might use four to six sets for 1 to 5 repetitions in the range of 65 to 85 percent based on 1RM values. Sets and repetitions are not arbitrary or varied for muscle confusion but are geared to enable the athlete to meet the goal of the training session.

As for sequencing, resistance sessions should include high-priority or major exercises, trunk and stability exercises, and exercises for corrective purposes, stability, and dynamic mobility. In the sample program tables 10.7 through 10.9, the first exercise in each superset is a high-priority or major exercise, the second exercise is a trunk or stability exercise, and the third exercise is corrective or works on stability or dynamic mobility.

The rationale for the superset pairings in this sequence is to minimize wasted time. In most of the program, the major exercise requires three minutes of recovery if the athlete is working in a repetition range geared to strength or power. Instead of simply resting for three minutes, however, the martial artist can perform two other exercises that do not deplete the same fuel source based on the intensity and priority of the muscles worked. While performing these second and third exercises, the athlete experiences active recovery for two or three minutes, which allows him or her to return to the high-priority exercise once the set is done.

Typical resistance sessions consist of an exercise pool of lower-body (for example, power cleans or squats), upper-body-push major exercises (bench press), and upper-body-pull major exercises (pull-ups). This pool provides plenty of choices so that the coach and martial artist can pick the best exercises based on the athlete's abilities or limitations (e.g., injury history, exercise experience). The second and third exercises are geared to complementary and noncompetitive goals in order to maximize the rest time for all of the major exercises for a given session. Table 10.3 lists some of the major exercises presented in earlier chapters, table 10.4 lists some secondary exercises, and table 10.5 lists some tertiary exercises.

Table 10.3   Primary Resistance Exercises

Monday	Wednesday	Friday
1 (a) Squat × 5, p. 49	1 (a) Flat bench press × 5, p. 100	1 (a) Clean and jerk × 5, p. 106
2 (a) Bent-over row × 5, p. 131	2 (a) Deadlift × 5, p. 130	2 (a) Hip thrust × 5, p. 110
3 (a) Flat bench press × 5, p. 100	3 (a) Pull-up × 5, p. 133	3 (a) Split-stance standing shoulder press × 5, p. 105
4 (a) Walking lunge × 5 each leg, p. 134	4 (a) Plyometric push-up × 5, p. 109	4 (a) Squat (dumbbell) × 5, p. 99
4 (b) Single-arm dumbbell row × 5, p. 135	4 (b) Double-leg buck × 5, p. 96	4 (b) Flat bench press × 5, p. 100
4 (c) Plyometric push-up × 5, p. 109	4 (c) Bent-over row × 5, p. 131	4 (c) Single-arm dumbbell row × 5, p. 135

Table 10.4   Secondary Resistance Exercises

Monday	Wednesday	Friday
1 (b) Three plank positions 20 to 30 sec., p. 91	1 (b) Single-leg hip thrust (variation) × 12, p. 111	1 (b) Kneeling ISO hold 20 sec. each side, p. 95
2 (b) Three plank positions 20 to 30 sec., p. 91	2 (b) Tall monster walk × 12 each leg, p. 95	2 (b) Bent-over T × 12, p. 54
3 (b) Glute–ham ISO hold 20 to 30 sec., p. 96	3 (b) Physioball roll-out × 12, p. 93	3 (b) Elbow tap × 8 each side, p. 124

Table 10.5   Tertiary Resistance Exercises

Monday	Wednesday	Friday
1 (c) Bent-over T × 12, p. 54	1 (c) Three plank positions 20 to 45 sec., p. 91	1 (c) Cat/cow × 12, p. 39
2 (c) Tall monster walk × 12 each leg, p. 95	2 (c) Bent-over 90/90 × 12, p. 55	2 (c) Tall monster walk (backward) × 12 each leg, p. 95
3 (c) Elbow tap × 8 each side, p. 124	3 (c) Tall monster walk (forward) × 12 each leg, p. 95	3 (c) Side-lying abduction × 12 each side, p. 42

Using the exercises that appear in the previous chapters, you can customize a training program for kicking and striking. The exercise sequence should go like this: All major exercises are paired with secondary and tertiary exercise choices for the first three supersets. Once the martial artist gets to the fourth superset, only primary exercises are performed. This approach allows the practitioner to perform one more set of all the major movements from lower body, upper pull, and upper push for more exercise stimulus. Having them set aside as a possible primary-only final set gives the athlete the option to either perform these lifts or exclude them, depending on fatigue and the calendar of events.

Take care not to add too much exercise variation too frequently. Sets and repetitions should change weekly, but too many variables make it more challenging for the body to adapt and exercise selection should remain somewhat stable. A good rule of thumb is to make changes in exercise selection with each mesocycle (month) of training. Also, even though this chapter addresses striking and kicking, these exercises may also be good selections for grappling and wrestling.

Recovery

As with the warm-up, the recovery can be approached by means of any number of strategies. For example, if the workout day is over, spending 10 to 15 minutes in a whirlpool can be a good way to help recover as it will help the body relax. On the other hand, if the athlete has another training bout that day, a cold plunge may better aid recovery and readiness for the next session to avoid too much relaxation. Hot and cold contrast showers can also serve as a great postworkout recovery strategy leading into the next training session. Another great postsession strategy is to use soft-tissue massage or foam rolling paired with active isolated stretching (AIS). Table 10.6 lists some recovery strategies distributed across a sample week; for more information about recovery methods, see chapter 8.

All recovery sessions should be done either after a practice session or, when additional recovery is needed, in place of a practice session. The athlete must take responsibility for her or his own training and manage fatigue as well as possible. In doing so, it is never a bad idea to take a conservative approach by erring on the side of more recovery.

Morning recovery sessions should be done after training with the assumption that another practice or workout may be performed later in the day. For this reason, morning recovery strategies never use heat alone. Afternoon sessions, in contrast, are approached with the assumption that no other practice will be done that day; therefore, any of the recovery methods can be used.

Table 10.6   Recovery Strategies

	Morning	Afternoon	Evening
Monday	Cold plunge, p. 188	Foam roll, p. 186	AIS, p. 189 Recovery breathing, p. 188
Tuesday	Barefoot cool-down, p. 190	Contrast bath, p. 188	Foam roll, p. 186 Recovery breathing, p. 188
Wednesday	Hot and cold contrast bath, p. 188	Foam roll, p. 186	AIS, p. 189 Recovery breathing, p. 188
Thursday	Cold plunge, p. 188	Barefoot cool-down, p. 190	Foam roll, p. 186 Recovery breathing, p. 188
Friday	Foam roll, p. 186 Barefoot cool-down, p. 190	Contrast bath, p. 188	AIS, p. 189 Recovery breathing, p. 188
Saturday	AIS, p. 189 Cold plunge, p. 188	Foam roll, p. 186	Hot bath, p. 188 Recovery breathing, p. 188
Sunday	Off		

SAMPLE PROGRAM

Here is a sample program for a martial artist; the key lies in the sequencing. The old adage that an athlete's preparation predicts his or her performance holds true in tactical sessions as well as strength and conditioning sessions. This particular program rests on four pillars: active dynamic warm-up, movement sessions (speed or agility), resistance (strength) training, and cool-down or active recovery. If performed with good intent, the workout should last about 65 or 70 minutes. If there is not time to perform a complete warm-up, the workout quality suffers, and the risk of injury increases.

This outline is ideal regardless of training level (beginner, intermediate, or advanced), but accountability ultimately rests on the martial artist, depending on his or her current fitness. Be smart and remember that all the tactical training sessions must be taken into account. If the athlete is new to strength and conditioning, integrate it only on one day for the first couple of weeks. If this addition does not impair tactical practices, integrate it on more days. However, avoid adding more than three days per week, because the accumulation of workload might impair performance. Always err on the side of doing less rather than more.

In the sample program, Monday's session consists of these four elements:

1. Full, active, dynamic warm-up (10 minutes)
2. Movement—speed drills (10 minutes)
3. Resistance training (40 minutes)
4. Cool-down or active recovery (10 minutes)

More specific details are provided for Monday's session in table 10.7.

Table 10.7   Sample Program for Striking and Kicking: Monday

	Exercise	Sets and reps
Active dynamic warm-up	Quadruped series, p. 35 Straight-leg series, p. 41 Dynamic flexibility, p. 56 Linear skip, p. 67	
Speed drills	Wall drill one-count, p. 158	5 reps
	Wall drill two-count, p. 159	5 reps × 2 sets (left and right)
	Wall drill three-count, p. 160	5 reps
	Sprints, short acceleration, p. 20; 60 sec. rest between sprints and 2 min. rest between sets	2 sets × 3 reps at 10 yards

Resistance	Superset 1:
	  Squat, p. 49
	  Plank, p. 91
	  Bent-over T, p. 54
	  Rest (60 sec.)
		3 × 5
		3 × 30 sec.
		3 × 12

	Superset 2:
	  Pull-up, p. 133
	  Elbow tap, p. 124
	  Cat/cow, p. 39
	  Rest (60 sec.)
		3 × 5
		3 × 6 each arm
		3 × 8

	Superset 3:
	  Flat bench press, p. 100
	  Tall monster walk, p. 95
	  Single-leg hip thrust (variation), p. 111
	  Rest (60 sec.)
		3 × 5
		3 × 10 each side
		3 × 6 each leg

	Superset 4:
	  Bent-over row, p. 131
	  Plyometric push-up, p. 109
	  Elbow tap, p. 124
	  Rest (60 sec.)
		3 × 5
		3 × 5 each side
		3 × 6 each side

Recovery	Foam roll, p. 186 Active isolated stretching (AIS), p. 189 Contrast bath, p. 188	

Wednesday's session consists of these four elements:

1. Full, active, dynamic warm-up (10 minutes)
2. Movement—agility and footwork (15 minutes)
3. Resistance training (30 minutes)
4. Cool-down or active recovery (10 minutes)

More specific details are provided for Wednesday's session in table 10.8.

Table 10.8   Sample Program for Striking and Kicking: Wednesday

	Exercise	Sets and reps
Active dynamic warm-up	Quadruped series, p. 35 Straight-leg series, p. 41 Squat series, p. 48 Dynamic flexibility, p. 56 Carioca, p. 66	
Agility and footwork	Line hop, p. 169	3 × 6 to 8 sec.
	In and out, p. 70	3 × 6 to 8 sec.
	Hip rotation, pp. 152, 168	3 × 6 to 8 sec.
	Box drill, p. 172	4
	Pro shuttle, p. 21	4

Resistance	Superset 1:
	    Vertical jump without countermovement, p. 16
	    Three plank positions (side), p. 91
	    Toe tap, p. 60
	    Rest (60 sec.)
		3 × 5
		3 × 20 each side
		3 × 5 each side

	Superset 2:
	    Broad jump with countermovement, p. 18
	    Medicine-ball rotational throw, p. 118
	    Plyometric push-up hold, p. 109
	    Rest (60 sec.)
		3 × 5
		3 × 5 each side
		3 × 30 sec.

	Superset 3:
	    Clean and jerk, p. 106
	    Side-lying abduction, p. 42
	    Rest (2 min.)
		3 × 5
		3 × 5 each side

	Superset 4:
	    Push-up plus, p. 103
	    Single-leg hip thrust (variation), p. 111
	    Single-arm dumbbell row, p. 135
	    Rest (60 sec.)
		3 × 5 each side
		3 × 10
		3 × 5 each side

Recovery	Barefoot cool-down, p. 190 Contrast bath (hot and cold), p. 188	

Friday's session consists of these four elements:

1. Full, active, dynamic warm-up (10 minutes)
2. Movement—speed and lateral speed (10 minutes)
3. Resistance training (40 minutes)
4. Cool-down or active recovery (10 minutes)

More specific details are provided for Friday's session in table 10.9.

Table 10.9 Sample Program for Striking and Kicking: Friday

	Exercise	Sets and reps
Active dynamic warm-up	Dynamic flexibility, p. 56 Quadruped series, p. 35 Straight-leg series, p. 41 Shoulder series, p. 53 Squat series, p. 48	
Speed and lateral speed	Bullet-belt partner march, p. 162 Rest (60 sec.) between sets	3 × 10 yards
	Bullet-belt partner-resisted run, p. 102 Rest (90 sec.) between sets	3 × 5 yards
	Box drill, p. 172 Rest (45 sec.) between sets	1 × 4
	Carioca, p. 66	2 × 25 yards
Resistance	Superset 1: Deadlift, p. 130 Kneeling ISO hold, p. 95 Elbow tap, p. 124 Rest (2 min.)	3 × 5 3 × 20 each side 3 × 5 each side
	Superset 2: Pull-up, p. 133 Rear-foot elevated split squat, p. 104 Plank, p. 91 Rest (60 sec.)	3 × 5 3 × 6 each side 3 × 8
	Superset 3: Landmine row to punch, p. 108 Open-stance medicine-ball throw, p. 142 Toe tap, p. 60 Rest (60 sec.)	3 × 6 each side 3 × 6 each side 3 × 6 each side
	Superset 4: Flat bench press, p. 100 Landmine row, p. 132 Physioball push-up hold, p. 94 Rest (60 sec.)	3 × 6 3 × 6 each side 3 × 30 sec.

	Exercise	Sets and reps
Recovery	Foam roll, p. 186 Active isolated stretching (AIS), p. 189 Barefoot cool-down, p. 190 Contrast bath (1:1 hot and cold), p. 188	

CONCLUSION

The goal of this chapter is to give athletes the autonomy to build their own schedule based on individual needs and circumstances. The next chapter resembles this one in the way in which programs are laid out, but the exercise selection is more specific to grappling and wrestling.

Chapter **11**

Programs for the Wrestling and Grappling Arts

Just as chapter 10 is dedicated to the striking and kicking martial artist, chapter 11 focuses on the wrestling and grappling practitioner. Even so, the exercises highlighted in this chapter may also be useful for a striking and kicking athlete. A needs analysis for a wrestler or grappler shows both general qualities and specific qualities that give the athlete the edge in a match. General qualities that best prepare an athlete for competition are speed, strength, power, endurance, and flexibility. However, a wrestler or grappler must also address specific needs, including grip strength and grip endurance, neck strength, and trunk strength.

Table 11.1 provides a quick reference guide to the rounds, minutes per round, and primary demands faced by athletes in sports based on grappling and wrestling. It could be argued that the demands, such as endurance, are a priority for each discipline, but we must recognize that all the demands compliment others for a given sport.

Developing both general and specific qualities is critical for success. To determine which areas an athlete needs to work on, use the testing process covered in chapter 2. Remember to not confuse skill success with resistance training capability. For example, a person could be a black belt in his or her discipline but a white belt, so to speak, in terms of strength and conditioning.

The best way to work on the needed qualities is to set the foundation with a broad base of muscular endurance. This process is aided by phase potentiation (figure 11.1), which involves using one block of training to build toward the next block.

Table 11.1 Demands of Wrestling, Judo, and Brazilian Jiu-Jitsu

Sport	Time/round	Speed	Strength	Power	Endurance
Wrestling	Round 1: 3 min. Round 2: 2 min. Round 3: 2 min.	Yes	Yes	Yes	Yes
Judo	5 min. 3 min. golden score (overtime)	Yes	Yes	Yes	Yes
Brazilian jiu-jitsu	White 5 min. Blue 6 min. Purple 7 min. Brown 8 min. Black 10 min.	Yes	Yes	Yes	Yes

Figure 11.1   Phase potentiation.

Muscular endurance must be built at the start of training and maintained for in-season success. Uniquely, a majority of the pure conditioning done by a grappling athlete takes place during practice sessions. It is easy to overdo conditioning, and the athlete must use common sense in determining which training quality is most ignored and which approach makes best use of time and attention for strength and conditioning. For example, most athletes will spend entire tactical sessions where major amounts of conditioning are being developed and then turn their second training session into conditioning, when perhaps a better use of the second session could be strength, power, and speed development.

Again, skill and tactical sessions must be given priority. If strength and conditioning sessions inhibit good practice habits, the athlete must switch the schedule to best maximize skills training. If the athlete has too much fatigue from strength and conditioning work, they may suffer in tactical sessions due to fatigue. It is important to remember that the development of skill in the tactical sessions is what's priority for the athlete. For most athletes, it is ideal to undertake a strength and conditioning program that takes place on two or three days per week.

The weekly breakdown presented in this chapter is purely an example of how training sessions can be organized and structured; it should not be viewed as *the* program. To best ensure positive training results, use the evaluation process described in chapter 2 to identify individual strengths and weaknesses and address the keys to performance for each discipline. A sound evaluation process helps clarify the training plan and best prepares the martial artist to meet goals.

BUILDING AN EFFECTIVE PROGRAM

Exercise selection and daily training theme are subject to the discretion of the practitioner based on testing results, sport-specific needs analysis, time of year, and the athlete's training age (exposure to physical preparation). The four categories of training are as follows: active dynamic warm up; skill or movement emphasis for the day; resistance training (adjusted for the current block of training on the basis of endurance, strength, power, or speed); and recovery (based on methods and resources discussed in chapter 8). To start building an individualized program, use the previous chapters as a reference guide and as a quick menu of options for exercise selection and modalities.

Depending on the martial artist's individual needs, you might make a trade-off between resistance training and more general conditioning after a resistance training session. In most cases, I would rather see any additional conditioning added to the end of a tactical session. After a hard tactical session, it may not be a bad idea to end with 20 minutes of low-intensity aerobic conditioning; doing so aids the recovery of the harder session but also allows the athlete to preserve the aerobic foundation as training intensities increase.

After a light drilling session, it might be a good time to add a short burst of intensive exercise, such as a Tabata interval. In contrast, trying to do a Tabata interval after a hard practice results in poor effort; the athlete may work hard due to accumulated fatigue, but the quality of work is sacrificed. Implementing this strategy of Tabata intervals after a light session provides the martial artist with a good way to maximize effort and quality while distributing the workload, because the intensive bouts takes only 3 or 4 minutes of the overall practice time of 30 to 45 minutes.

Active Dynamic Warm-Up

To build the warm-up, pick three to five series each day. Table 11.2 lists some featured warm-up exercises. The warm-up can be nearly the same each day, which enables the athlete to learn and master the movements, thus developing better range of motion throughout the movement. Alternatively, the sequences can be varied as often as one likes. Either way, the goal is to get comfortable and prepare the body for the movement session that follows.

Table 11.2   Selected Warm-Ups

Monday	Wednesday	Friday
Quadruped series, p. 35	Squat series, p. 48	Straight-leg series, p. 41
Straight-leg series, p. 41	Shoulder series, p. 53	Squat series, p. 48
Dynamic flexibility, p. 56	Quadruped series, p. 35	Quadruped series, p. 35
Shoulder series, p. 53	Straight-leg series , p. 41	Dynamic flexibility, p. 56
Squat series, p. 48	Carioca, p. 66	Shoulder series, p. 53

Movement

The movement emphasis can change daily, but linear speed development may not be the best use of time for a wrestler or grappler. For this reason, the movement emphasis will be either footwork or agility, which are two separate qualities. Choose three or four drills each day and perform two or three repetitions with plenty of recovery time. The focus here is not on conditioning but on movement quality; avoid accumulating too much fatigue. Table 11.3 lists featured exercises from throughout the chapters.

Table 11.3   Selected Drills for Movement Emphasis

Monday	Wednesday	Friday
Lateral hurdle run, p. 172	Medicine-ball toe touch, p. 170	Line hop, p. 169
Shuffle drills (lateral speed shuffle, partner reactive shuffle, side shuffle), pp. 174, 148, 69	Carioca, p. 66	Hip rotation, pp. 152, 168
Spider drill, p. 23	Partner reactive shuffle, p. 148	Box drill, p. 172

Resistance

The resistance training emphasis can be adjusted in terms of repetitions and percent of effort on weight lifted. For example, if the goal is muscular endurance, you might use two or three sets of 12 to 15 repetitions or more in an intensity range of 60 percent to 70 percent effort based on 1-repetition max (1RM). If the goal is strength, you might use three to five sets of 1 to 5 repetitions in an intensity range of 80 percent to 100 percent effort based on 1RM values. And if the goal is power development, you might use four to six sets of 1 to 5 repetitions in the range of 65 percent to 85 percent based on 1RM values. Sets and repetitions are not arbitrary or varied for muscle confusion but are geared to enable the athlete to meet the goal of the training session.

As for sequencing, resistance sessions should include high-priority or major exercises, trunk and stability exercises, and exercises for corrective purposes, stability, and dynamic mobility. In the sample program tables 11.8 through 11.10, the first exercise in each superset is a high-priority or major exercise, the second exercise is a trunk or stability exercise, and the third exercise is corrective or works on stability or dynamic mobility.

The rationale for the pairings of supersets 1a, 1b, and 1c in table 11.4 is to minimize wasted time. In most of the program, the major exercise requires three minutes of recovery if the athlete is working in a repetition range geared to strength or power. Instead of simply resting for three minutes, however, the martial artist can perform two other exercises that do not deplete the same fuel source based on the intensity and priority of the muscles worked. While performing these second and third exercises, the athlete experiences active recovery for two or three minutes, which allows him or her to return to the high-priority exercise once the set is done.

Typical resistance sessions consist of an exercise pool of lower-body (for example, squats) or total-body major exercises (power or hang cleans), upper-body-push major exercises (bench press), and upper-body-pull major exercises (pull-up). This pool provides plenty of choices so that the coach and martial artist can pick the best exercises based on the athlete's abilities or limitations (e.g., injury history, exercise experience). The second and third exercises are geared to complementary and noncompetitive goals in order to maximize the rest time for all the major exercises for a given session. Table 11.4 lists some of the major exercises presented in earlier chapters, table 11.5 lists some secondary exercises, and table 11.6 lists some tertiary exercises.

Table 11.4 Primary Resistance Exercises

Monday	Wednesday	Friday
1 (a) Deadlift × 5, p. 130	1 (b) Overhead medicine-ball throw × 5, p. 117	1 (c) Zercher squat × 5, p. 138
2 (a) Pull-up × 5, p. 133	2 (b) Clean and jerk × 5, p. 106	2 (c) Flat bench press × 5, p. 100
3 (a) Heavy-bag carry × 30 sec., p. 136	3 (b) Fat-grip horizontal row × 5, p. 137	3 (c) Pull-up × 5, p. 133
4 (a) Single-leg hip thrust (variation) × 5, p. 111	4 (a) Farmer walk × 45 sec., p. 135	4 (a) Walking lunge × 5 each leg, p. 134
4 (b) Landmine row × 5, p. 132	4 (b) Tall monster walk (backward) × 12, p. 95	4 (b) Toe tap × 30 sec., p. 125
4 (c) Physioball push-up hold × 30 sec., p. 94	4 (c) Towel curl to press (slow and deliberate) × 15, p. 98	4 (c) Battle-rope drumming × 30 sec., p. 127

Table 11.5 Secondary Resistance Exercises

Monday	Wednesday	Friday
1 (b) Elbow tap × 5 each side, p. 124	1 (b) Partner medicine-ball drop × 5, p. 120	1 (b) Medicine-ball broad jump × 3, p. 145
2 (b) Three plank positions (side) × 20 to 30 sec., p. 90	2 (b) Dumbbell squat jump × 5, p. 119	2 (b) Partner medicine-ball drop × 5, p. 120
3 (b) Tall monster walk (side) × 10 each side, p. 95	3 (b) Physioball partner push × 20 to 30 sec., p. 126	3 (b) Open-stance medicine-ball throw × 5 each side, p. 142

Table 11.6 Tertiary Resistance Exercises

Monday	Wednesday	Friday
1 (c) Supine neck lift × 10, p. 97	1 (c) Closed-stance medicine-ball throw × 5 each side, p. 143	1 (c) Cat/cow × 8, p. 39
2 (c) Physioball partner push × 30 sec., p. 126	2 (c) Stir the pot × 5 each direction, p. 126	2 (c) Side-lying abduction × 5 each side, p. 42
3 (c) Three plank positions (prone) × 20 to 30 sec., p. 90	3 (c) Glute–ham ISO hold × 10 to 20 sec., p. 96	3 (c) Three plank positions (prone) × 20 to 30 sec., p. 90

Using the exercises that appear in the previous chapters, you can customize a training program for grappling and wrestling. The exercise sequence should go like this: All major exercises are paired with secondary and tertiary exercise choices for the first three supersets. Once the martial artist gets to the fourth superset, only primary exercises are performed. This approach allows the athlete to perform one more lower-body and upper-body-pull and upper-body-push exercise for more stimulus (or workload) depending on the phase of training the athlete is currently in and the calendar of events. Having them set aside a possible primary-only final set gives the athlete the option to either perform these lifts or exclude them, depending on fatigue and the calendar of events.

Take care not to add too much exercise variation too frequently; the athlete is in the process of mastering these skills for more efficient execution over time. Sets and repetitions should change weekly, but exercise selection should remain somewhat stable. A good rule of thumb is to make changes in exercise selection with each mesocycle (month) of training. Also, even though this chapter addresses grappling and wrestling, these exercises would also be good selections for kicking and striking.

Recovery

As with the warm-up, the recovery can be approached by means of any number of strategies. For example, if the workout day is over, spending 10 to 15 minutes in a whirlpool can be a good way to recover. On the other hand, if the athlete has another training bout that day, a cold plunge may better aid recovery and readiness for the next session. Hot and cold contrast showers can also serve as a great postworkout recovery strategy leading into the next training session. Another great postsession recovery strategy is to use soft-tissue massage or foam rolling, paired with active isolated stretching (AIS). Table 11.7 lists some recovery strategies distributed across a sample week; for more information about recovery methods, see chapter 8.

Table 11.7 Recovery Strategies

	Morning	Afternoon	Evening
Monday	Cold bath, p. 188	Foam rolling, p. 186	AIS, p. 189 Recovery breathing, p. 188
Tuesday	Barefoot cool-down, p. 190	Contrast bath, p. 188	Foam roll, p. 186 Recovery breathing, p. 188
Wednesday	Contrast bath, p. 188	Foam roll, p. 186	AIS, p. 189 Recovery breathing, p. 188
Thursday	Cold bath, p. 188	Barefoot cool-down, p. 190	Foam roll, p. 186 Recovery breathing, p. 188
Friday	Foam roll, p. 186 Barefoot cool-down, p. 190	Cold bath, p. 188	AIS, p. 189 Recovery breathing, p. 188
Saturday	AIS, p. 189 Cold bath, p. 188	Foam roll, p. 186	Hot bath, p. 188 Recovery breathing, p. 188
Sunday	Off		

All recovery sessions should be done either after the practice session or, when additional recovery is needed, in place of a practice session. The athlete must take responsibility for her or his own training and manage fatigue as well as possible. In doing so, it is never a bad idea to take a conservative approach by erring on the side of more recovery.

Morning recovery sessions should be done after training with the assumption that another practice or workout may be performed later in the day. For this reason, morning recovery strategies never use heat alone. Afternoon sessions, in contrast, are approached with the assumption that no other practice will be done that day; therefore, any of the recovery methods can be used.

SAMPLE PROGRAM

This program is presented only as a sample to help you understand the time needed for each pillar of the training day: active dynamic warm-up, movement sessions (footwork and agility), resistance (strength) training, and cool-down or active recovery. The sequence in which these qualities are trained is the priority.

In the sample program, Monday's session consists of these four elements:

1. Full, active, dynamic warm-up (10 minutes)
2. Footwork emphasis (10 minutes)
3. Resistance training (30 to 40 minutes)
4. Cool-down and regeneration (10 minutes)

More specific details are provided for Monday's session in table 11.8. Wednesday's session consists of these four elements:

1. Full, active, dynamic warm-up (10 minutes)
2. Footwork and agility (10 minutes)
3. Resistance training (30 to 40 minutes)
4. Cool-down and regeneration (10 minutes)

More specific details are provided for Wednesday's session in table 11.9.

Friday's session consists of these four elements:

1. Active, dynamic, warm-up (10 minutes)
2. Footwork and agility (10 minutes)
3. Resistance training (30 to 40 minutes)
4. Cool-down and regeneration (10 minutes)

More specific details are provided for Friday's session in table 11.10.

Table 11.8 Sample Program for Wrestling and Grappling: Monday

	Exercise	Sets and reps
Active dynamic warm-up	Squat series, p. 48 Hip rotation series, p. 45 Quadruped series, p. 35 Shoulder series, p. 53	
Footwork and agility	Lateral hurdle run, p. 172	6 sets × 4 reps (1:1 work-to-rest ratio)
	Line hop, p. 169	1 × 3 (1:1 work-to-rest ratio)
	In and out, p. 70	1 × 3 (1:1 work-to-rest ratio)
	Hip rotation, p. 152	1 × 3 (1:1 work-to-rest ratio)
Resistance	Superset 1: 　Deadlift, p. 130 　Elbow tap, p. 124 　Supine neck lift, p. 97 　Rest (2 to 3 min.)	3 × 5 3 × 5 each 3 × 12
	Superset 2: 　Pull-up, p. 133 　Three plank positions (side), p. 90 　Physioball partner push, p. 126 　Rest (2 to 3 min.)	3 × 5 3 × 20 sec. each side 3 × 5 sec. each side
	Superset 3: 　Heavy-bag carry, p. 136 　Tall monster walk, p. 95 　Toe touch, p. 60 　Rest (2 to 3 min.)	3 × 20 sec. 3 × 12 each side 3 × 6 each side
	Superset 4: 　Single-leg hip thrust (variation), p. 111 　Landmine row, p. 132 　Physioball push-up hold, p. 94 　Rest (60 to 90 sec.)	3 × 6 each side 3 × 6 3 × 30 sec.
Recovery	Barefoot cool-down, p. 190 Active isolated stretching (AIS), p. 189 Cold bath, p. 188	

Table 11.9 Sample Program for Wrestling and Grappling: Wednesday

	Exercise	Sets and reps
Active dynamic warm-up	Squat series, p. 48 Shoulder series, p. 53 Dynamic flexibility, p. 56 Hip rotation series, p. 45	
Footwork and agility	Medicine-ball toe touch, p. 170	5 × 30 sec., 15 sec. rest between sets
	Side shuffle, p. 69	4 × 15 yards or meters (1:1 work-to-rest ratio
	Carioca, p. 66	4 × 20 yards or meters (1:1 work-to-rest ratio)
	Spider drill, p. 23	2 (1:1 work-to-rest ratio)

Resistance	Superset 1:
	    Overhead medicine-ball throw, p. 117
	    Partner medicine-ball drop, p. 120
	    Closed-stance medicine-ball throw, p. 143
	    Rest (60 sec.)
		
		3 × 5
		3 × 5
		3 × 5 each side

	Superset 2:
	    Clean and jerk, p. 106
	    Dumbbell squat jump (light), p. 119
	    Stir the pot, p. 126
	    Rest (2 to 3 min.)
		
		3 × 5
		3 × 5
		3 × 5 each direction

	Superset 3:
	    Fat-grip horizontal row, p. 137
	    Physioball partner push, p. 126
	    Glute–ham ISO hold, p. 96
	    Rest (60 to 90 sec.)
		
		3 × 6
		3 × 30 sec.
		3 × 6

	Superset 4:
	    Farmer walk, p. 135
	    Tall monster walk (backward), p. 95
	    Towel curl to press, p. 98
	    Rest (60 to 90 sec.)
		
		3 × 45 sec.
		3 × 10 each side
		3 × 15 slow tempo

Recovery	Active isolated stretching (AIS), p. 189 Contrast bath, p. 188 Recovery breathing, p. 188	

Table 11.10 Sample Program for Wrestling and Grappling: Friday

	Exercise	Sets and reps
Active dynamic warm-up	Quadruped series, p. 35 Straight-leg series, p. 41 Squat series, p. 48 Dynamic flexibility, p. 56	
Footwork and agility	Lateral speed shuffle, p. 174	1 set x 6 to 8 reps (1:3 work-to-rest ratio)
	Partner reactive shuffle, p. 148	2 sets × 3 reps (10 sec.; 1:3 work-to-rest ratio)
	In and out, p. 153	1set × 4 reps (8 sec.; 1:3 work-to-rest ratio)

Resistance	Superset 1:
	  Zercher squat, p. 138
	  Medicine-ball broad jump, p. 145
	  Cat/cow, p. 39
	  Rest (2 to 3 min.)
		
		3 × 5
		3 × 3
		3 × 8

	Superset 2:
	  Flat bench press, p. 100
	  Partner medicine-ball drop, p. 120
	  Side-lying abduction (slow), p. 42
	  Rest (2 to 3 min.)
		
		3 × 5
		3 × 5
		3 × 5 each side

	Superset 3:
	  Pull-up, p. 133
	  Open-stance medicine-ball throw, p. 142
	  Three plank positions (prone), p. 90
	  Rest (2 to 3 min.)
		
		3 × 5
		3 × 6 each side
		3 × 30 sec.

	Superset 4:
	  Walking lunge, p. 134
	  Toe tap, p. 125
	  Battle-rope drumming, p. 127
	  Rest (60 to 90 sec.)
		
		3 × 5 each side
		3 × 30 sec.
		3 × 30 sec.

Recovery	Foam roll, p. 189 Active isolated stretching (AIS), p. 189 Barefoot cool-down, p. 190	

CONCLUSION

The goal of this chapter is to give athletes the autonomy to build their schedule based on individual needs and circumstances. In the next chapter, you will see individual needs really come into play, because there are multiple disciplines (as well as strength and conditioning) to master. Avoid adding too much to the schedule and never hesitate to remove a session from the strength and conditioning column in order to enable further mastery of the chosen martial art.

Chapter 12

Blending and Customizing Programs for MMA

So far, the journey of working through this book has shown you that even as martial arts disciplines share many similarities, they also differ in distinct ways that make each discipline unique. With that said, there must be a chapter on training for mixed martial arts (MMA), though in truth I could write an entire book on the subject.

MMA has become one of the fastest-growing sports in recent years. Part of the reason lies in the fact that one-on-one combat truly defines pure competition. In addition, the blend of disciplines used in MMA makes it popular around the globe. This blend also makes it tricky to implement strength and conditioning programs for MMA due to the sport's diverse tactical training demands. As noted throughout this book, training must prioritize skill acquisition and proficiency in the chosen martial art. In the case of MMA, training must also account for multiple disciplines, which makes organization and planning your biggest allies.

In MMA, amateur fights are typically scheduled for three rounds of three minutes each with one minute of rest between rounds. Professional fights are scheduled for either three or five rounds (five for title fights) of five minutes each with one minute of rest between rounds. These demands require that we blend the qualities described in this book. For example, striking must be fast and explosive, whereas grappling requires strength, power, and major muscular endurance. Essentially, then, a blend of the strength methods addressed in chapters 10 and 11 covers the basics for most MMA fighters.

As a coach to more than 50 MMA athletes, I have learned the importance of understanding the training age of my clients—as well as the weekly demands of their skill sessions—when building MMA training programs. A common mistake made by athletes who are new to the sport involves the belief that strength and conditioning will give them their edge in the cage or the octagon. The truth, however, is that strength and conditioning are simply the icing on the cake, which is made primarily of the cultivated skills. No number of power cleans or Tabata intervals will allow someone to out-prepare another fighter who possesses a drastic skill advantage, so please make sure that these workouts are complementary rather than hindering to tactical sessions.

In this chapter, I approach programming for MMA based on my own perspective. Please understand that no two circumstances, training camps, or athletes are ever the same. With that reality in mind, use this chapter as a reference and a guide based on various training strategies and camp situations.

The challenge boils down to organizing the training schedule and determining which type of training to prioritize during which part of the competitive year for each individual fighter. Most MMA teams train three high-priority disciplines throughout the week: striking (Muay Thai, kickboxing, boxing), wrestling, and Brazilian jiu-jitsu. These practice sessions may be associated with a drilling or technical emphasis or a live session. An athlete may also engage in one or two sparring days per week. Most teams conduct two or three practices per day to cover all disciplines while alternating technical and live practice and sparring—thus adding up to 11 to 13 practices per week! In this busy schedule, where and how do we fit in strength and conditioning?

TIMING OF STRENGTH AND CONDITIONING TRAINING

Typically, an MMA athlete decides to begin a new strength and conditioning program upon the announcement of his or her next fight. This is the worst time to begin anything new. Most fight announcements are made with short notice (four to six weeks), and the last thing a fighter should do is add anything new into the training program that isn't tactically specific or aimed at helping the fighter stylistically with the upcoming opponent. The soreness and fatigue created by a new stimulus such as a strength and conditioning program would make it hard for the athlete to truly adapt to the change in training.

Instead, the optimal time to begin this new strategy is during the off-season, which is really more of a hypothetical term than a true transition in a season. Most MMA athletes feel the need to train year-round so that if the opportunity arises for a short-notice fight, their physical preparation allows them to engage in a short training camp. Still, the off-season is the best time to begin experimenting with a new strength and conditioning program.

SCHEDULE

In the master schedule, the practitioner lays out all potential practices and decides where to fit strength and conditioning work. Specifically, a determination must be made about when and how to begin a strength and conditioning program.

As shown in table 12.1, MMA athletes participate in as many as 11 practices per week, which creates a scheduling nightmare for athletes who don't take ownership of their own time. I suggest that athletes sit down with their head coaches and work together to determine the best days and times for strength and conditioning work. The head coach may support the idea of strength and conditioning training or may feel that the athlete gets all that he or she needs in tactical sessions. Regardless of the coach's perspective, however, the athlete needs to know how to integrate these sessions, as well as what the parameters of the sessions should be.

Table 12.1   Sample Schedule for an MMA Athlete

Practice	Monday	Tuesday	Wednesday	Thursday	Friday	Saturday	Sunday
Striking	×		×		×	×	Off
Brazilian jiu-jitsu and judo		×		×	×		Off
Wrestling	×		×				Off
Sparring		×				×	Off

COMMON MISTAKES

When faced with the intensive nature and restrictive time parameters of MMA, many athletes try to make all training sessions mimic the sport. They think that by using the standard round lengths and the one-minute recovery time between rounds they are building a training program that is specific to the mixed martial artist. This is not, however, the case.

The best way to help an MMA athlete add power to his or her training regimen is to build a program that gives the athlete what he or she isn't getting in tactical training sessions. Most tactical sessions start with good speed and power work that are sport specific. However, athletes often do not adhere to the work-to-rest intervals and time requirements that are essential for developing these performance qualities. As a result, many sessions default into elongated conditioning practices.

To avoid this pitfall, the MMA athlete needs to perform a critical analysis of what he or she is missing based on the requirements of athleticism. In my opinion, and based on my experiences, the biggest void in preparation tends to involve pure strength work or resistance training. Therefore, it is essential to reteach and retrain the athlete in the fundamentals of the weight room.

OFF-SEASON PREPARATION

For MMA athletes, the term "off-season training" is a bit of a misnomer. Most fights are announced on short notice, thus making it hard for the athlete to plan how much time is available for a specific block of training. Also, in many instances, a traditional periodization-training model can be canceled out based on conflicting training demands. For example, taking on a high lactate workload would interfere with efforts to fully develop aerobic fitness. Therefore, MMA athletes must pick their battles in planning physical and technical preparation.

In addition, most MMA athletes are part of a team, and even though they may not have an upcoming fight, they still have training partners with looming fights who need live bodies with whom to train. As a result, MMA athletes must be smart in choosing how many live goes or sparring sessions they participate in away from their own training camps. In fact, this is where injuries are the highest. Out of camp, fighters tend to go into a sparring session without the same mindfulness or physical preparation, which leads to poor technique that may lead to injury amidst the intensity and duration of sparring. To best avoid injury is why it is imperative to deliberately get back into training and add one or two practices per week instead of jumping right back in feet first with a full training schedule as most fighters typically do.

To create a more robust MMA athlete, we must first commit to the process, and the best time to do that is right after a fight. Once the athlete has taken the necessary time off from the gym, it is time to slowly reinstate a schedule with the new pieces. After a fight, many athletes make the mistake of jumping back in right where they left off. Instead, they should slowly progress back into training to allow the body to adapt week by week. The body needs a balance of parasympathetic and sympathetic stimulation (see chapter 8), whereas adding too much too soon puts the athlete back into the sympathetic state and runs the risk of overtraining syndrome. Fighters should take two weeks off after a fight in order to fully recover, both physically and mentally. Depending on how intensive the fight was, the athlete may need to take even more time off and consult with a physician before starting training again.

Once the athlete has been cleared, the first session should focus on steady-state cardio and strength training. If the athlete is new to strength work, it is imperative to maintain the current weight class unless he or she is looking to move up. The last thing you want to do is demand that the fighter make a more difficult weight cut.

The capacity block (table 12.2) and the strength endurance block (table 12.3) happen at the same time. The goal of the capacity block is to increase (i.e., make bigger) the aerobic gas tank; meanwhile, the strength block increases muscular endurance to provide more strength potential in later pure-strength blocks. As you will see, each strength session has a total-body focus. This is a good strategy for influencing total-body strength but minimizing isolated stimulation to best manage or offset hypertrophy. As the block continues after the first week, the number of exercises per emphasis can increase to two per emphasis.

As in the other programming chapters, high-priority or emphasis exercises are coupled with core exercises or active range-of-motion exercises performed during the typical rest cycles. Most likely, based on training age and typically limited exposure to resistance training, the athlete will have to learn new exercises, and it is important to use a weight that is challenging for the selected number of sets and repetitions. Remember, however, that going to failure is not the goal. The goal is to select a weight that challenges the athlete but keeps them within safe parameters. Table 12.4 provides a quick, easy reference to help the athlete and coach begin a strength and conditioning program. Table 12.5 lists a sample strength

Table 12.2   Capacity Block 1: Aerobic Base and Resistance Training (Off-Season)

Week	Days	Heart rate (beats per min.)	Duration (min.)	Mode
1	Mon, Wed, Fri	130	20	Bike, treadmill, rower
2	Mon, Wed, Fri	130 to 140	30 to 40	Bike, treadmill, rower
3	Mon, Wed, Fri	140 to 150	45	Bike, treadmill, rower
4	Mon, Wed, Fri	140 to 150	60	Bike, treadmill, rower
Deload week	Mon, Fri	130 to 140	20 to 30	Bike, treadmill, rower

Table 12.3   Strength Endurance Block: Setting a Foundation (Off-Season)

Week	Days	Emphases	Exercises per emphasis	Sets and reps
1	Tues, Thurs	Push, pull, lower body	1:1:1	2 × 12 to 15
2	Tues, Thurs	Push, pull, lower body	2:2:2	2 × 12
3	Tues, Thurs	Push, pull, lower body	2:2:2	3 × 10
4	Tues, Thurs	Push, pull, lower body	2:2:2	4 × 8
Deload week	Tues, Thurs	Push, pull, lower body	1:1:1	2 × 8

endurance block for an easy guide of exercise options of primary, secondary, and tertiary exercises not unlike chapter 10 and 11.

To exercise some control and autonomy in exercise selection, the athlete can use the programs for striking and kicking presented in chapter 10 and the programs for grappling and wrestling presented in chapter 11 interchangeably.

Table 12.4 Days of the Week and Exercise Focus (Off-Season)

Week	Monday	Tuesday	Wednesday	Thursday	Friday	Saturday	Sunday
1	Cardio	Strength	Cardio	Strength	Cardio	Off	Off
2	Cardio	Strength	Cardio	Strength	Cardio	Off	Off
3	Cardio	Strength	Cardio	Strength	Cardio	Off	Off
4	Cardio	Strength	Cardio	Strength	Cardio	Off	Off
5	Cardio	Strength	Off	Strength	Cardio	Off	Off

Table 12.5 Sample Program: Strength Endurance Block (Week 1)

Tuesday (push, pull, lower; 1:1:1)	
Exercise	**Sets and reps**
Push-up, p. 102 Three plank positions (prone), p. 90 Bent-over T, p. 54 No rest	2 × 12 to 15 2 × 30 sec 2 × 12
Bent-over row, p. 131 Three plank positions (lateral), p. 90 Side-lying abduction, p. 42 No rest	2 × 12 to 15 2 × 15 sec per side 2 × 5 at 5 sec hold
Squat, p. 49 Physioball push-up hold, p. 94 Side lying abduction, p. 42 No rest	2 × 12 to 15 2 × 20 to 30 sec 2 × 5 per side
Thursday (lower, pull, push; 1:1:1)	
Zercher squat, p. 138 Get-up, p. 151 Bent-over T, p. 54 No rest	2 × 12 to 15 2 × 12 2 × 12
Single-arm dumbbell row, p. 135 Physioball push-up hold, p. 94 Tall monster walk, p. 95 No rest	2 × 12 to 15 2 × 15 to 30 sec 2 × 12 per side
Flat bench press, p. 100 Physioball roll-out, p. 93 Cat/cow, p. 39 No rest	2 × 12 to 15 2 × 10 2 × 6

* Bold indicates the high-priority exercise.

Now, if you haven't received the call for a fight or for the start of camp, you can go into capacity block 2 (table 12.6). The objective of block 2 is to increase the workload from the previous block.

Table 12.6 Capacity Block 2: Continued Aerobic-Capacity Work (Off-Season)

Week	Days	Heart rate (beats per min.)	Duration (min.)	Mode
6	Mon, Wed, Fri	130	30	Bike, treadmill, rower
7	Mon, Wed, Fri	130 to 140	35 to 45	Bike, treadmill, rower
8	Mon, Wed, Fri	135 to 145	45 to 60	Bike, treadmill, rower
9	Mon, Wed, Fri	140 to 150	60 to 80	Bike, treadmill, rower
Deload week	Tues, Thurs	130 to 140	30	Bike, treadmill, rower

Remember that capacity block 2 and strength block 2 (table 12.7) are done concurrently. The strength endurance block gives the athlete a better foundation on which to develop strength. If the athlete is new to strength work, it can be beneficial to do a couple of blocks of muscular endurance in succession in order to increase total resistance volume and thereby lay a better foundation. An athlete who has more resistance experience can typically perform one block of endurance and then move to the strength phase.

Table 12.7 Strength Block 2: First Strength Block After Muscular Endurance Block (Off-Season)

Week	Days	Emphasis	Exercises per emphasis	Sets and reps
6	Tues, Thurs	Push, pull, lower body	1:1:1	2 × 8
7	Tues, Thurs	Push, pull, lower body	2:1:1	3 × 6 to 8
8	Tues, Thurs	Push, pull, lower body	1:2:1	4 × 5
9	Tues, Thurs	Push, pull, lower body	1:1:2	5 × 5
Deload week	Tues, Thurs.	Push, pull, lower body	1:1:1	3 × 5

In week 7, two exercises are chosen for the main push emphasis for the day; in week 8, two exercises are used for the main pull emphasis; and in week 9, two exercises are selected for the main lower-body emphasis. This approach means, for example, that in week 9 you should have one pushing exercise (e.g., flat bench press), one pulling exercise (e.g., pull-up), and two exercise for the lower body (e.g., body-weight squat and walking lunge). This work creates the overload response that an MMA athlete needs from a new training stimulus without accumulating too much volume. An excess of volume can lead to hypertrophy and cause weight gain that may make a weight cut more difficult. To keep things under control, look for and note anthropometric changes that are excessive while consistently checking weight.

This completes the outline of how to structure training. To create the best plan for each athlete in each situation, take into account individual limitations and schedule differences. It takes time, and lots of tweaking, to find the best fit to maximize tactical sessions while providing a better base of fitness and strength to maximize the skill set. Athletes and coaches should communicate clearly about the program and which days are the best for strength and conditioning work. This planning is extremely important once the call arrives for a fight date.

IN CAMP

In camp, training must have the most specificity to the sport. For the MMA fighters I have worked with, weekly practices in camp are situated as shown in table 12.8. "Tech" refers to practice geared toward lower intensity with the main objective of grooving fundamental patterns for the specific discipline. "Live" refers to practice of highest intensity that is geared to put the technical skills into a performance tempo; it is very intense.

Table 12.8   Typical MMA Practice Schedule

Monday	Wrestling (live)	Striking (tech)	Strength and conditioning
Tuesday	Sparring (live)	Brazilian jiu-jitsu (tech)	
Wednesday	Wrestling (tech)	Strength and conditioning	
Thursday	Sparring (tech)	Brazilian jiu-jitsu (live)	
Friday	Striking (tech)	Strength and conditioning	
Saturday	Sparring (live)	Brazilian jiu-jitsu (tech	
Sunday	Off		

With this demanding schedule, it is easy for an athlete to wear down to the point of disrupting his or her training. Accountability here rests with the athlete to decide when to turn a typical strength and conditioning session into an active recovery session or a day off. Especially as calories tend to decrease, the fighter must understand that erring on the side of recovery is a better means to an effective camp.

During camp, I tend to retain one or two sessions of capacity work in order to help the athlete maintain the aerobic qualities gained during the off-season; the practice sessions take care of higher-intensity aerobic power and lactate-capacity work. I tend to see lactate power work, mainly in the fast glycolytic zones missed within most tactical training sessions. Highly intensive work that lasts 30 to 90 seconds with full recovery (using a work-to-rest ratio of 1:2 or 1:3) is typically lost in practices, because most tactical coaches do not pay much attention to shorter, more intense bursts with full rest. Based on my experience, most sessions drift into training aerobic power and capacity due to their duration and intensity. This drift poses a problem on fight night because the fighter has the needed aerobic capacity and lactate capacity but has failed to truly train lactate power.

If we step back and analyze a fight, we see that the fight is dynamic but that there are often positional changes from highly exhaustive positions (e.g., wrestling and grappling) to less intensive positions with more of an explosive need (e.g., striking and kicking). Implementing more fast-glycolytic interval work for power can help with those in-between demands for power that typically occur throughout a fight.

Earlier in this chapter, I showed a twice-weekly strength and conditioning plan; for the rest of the chapter, I will outline how I use strength and conditioning sessions during camp. Again, adapt this outline as you see fit, but I think you will find that I check off all the boxes for performance while situating sessions in a practical manner that allows the fighter to be at his or her best during sparring sessions, which is where the athlete must shine. Table 12.9 shows the weekly breakdown of in-camp training for my fighters.

Table 12.10 presents what is essentially an outline to help guide the athlete in camp; it should not be repeated exactly in its entirety. Make smart decisions based on training experience and the time and intensity of camp. Strength and conditioning should be viewed as icing on the cake of the overall program for an MMA athlete—especially during camp!

Table 12.9 Weekly Breakdown of Strength for MMA Training Camp

	Monday	Wednesday	Friday
Theme	**Alactic**	**Lactic**	**Aerobic**
Exercise modes and strategies	Short sprints Strength Power Contrast sprint Post-activation potentiation	Muscular endurance Supersets and giant sets (multiple exercises within a set) Metabolic circuit starting in week 3 of camp	Active recovery and steady-state circuit of low-intensity exercise for stability, strength, and active range of motion
Recovery	Full recovery to allow the ATP-PC system to prepare for repeated power and strength bouts	Recovery between sets Work-to-rest ratios: early camp 1:3, mid-camp 1:2, end of camp 1:1	No rest for the full workout: early camp 20 to 30 min. session, mid-camp 30 to 40 min. session, end of camp 20 min. session

Table 12.10 Monday: Alactic

Training mode	Theme	Exercise selections	Sets and reps	Rest and recovery
Sprints: Pick one drill from exercise selection.	High intent and explosive, high effort at 90% to 100%	10 and 20 yd. (m) sprints, p. 20 Acceleration wall drills Partner resistance runs (20 yds. or m), pp. 158, 84	2 or 3 × 3 or 4	2 or 3 min. between sets, 60 sec. between reps
Strength and power: Pick three or four exercises.	High effort and intent	Plyometric push-up, p. 109 Medicine ball throws, p. 142 Clean and jerk, p. 106	3 to 5 × 3 to 5	At least 3 min. recovery between sets
Conditioning: This is not a must and should be done only with submax effort.	Alactic-capacity effort at 75% to 85%	Repeated short sprints of 15 to 20 yds. (m), p. 116	2 or 3 × 4 to 6	60 to 90 sec. between sets or heart rate at 120 to 130 beats per min. Walk-back recovery between reps

During camp, the Wednesday session (table 12.11) is more metabolic yet specific to the window of 30 to 90 seconds of moderate to intensive effort. After going to all MMA practices for our fight team, I was able to study the work-to-rest ratios and determine where the athletes were missing important work zones. Many of the practices started off with high-intensity effort but, due to unrealistic work-to-rest ratios, I noticed a gap of specific conditioning in the fast-glycolytic range. Even though some of the intervals were aimed at speed and power for 10, 20 or even 30 seconds, the rest portion was insufficient to enable repeated power in those drills.

This realization prompted me to implement a quasi-metabolic day that stayed within those time and effort zones (fast glycolytic) while providing extensive recovery to allow repeated bursts of speed and power. At the beginning of camp, fighters get a 1:3 work-to-rest ratio; as conditioning levels rise, the ratio drops to 1:2 and sometimes 1:1, depending on the fighter's recovery rate. Rest is never sacrificed for effort!

Table 12.11 includes the term *shadow boxing*, which refers to the use of whatever footwork strategy the fighter uses during tactical sessions with the striking coach. The goal of shadow boxing is twofold. First, I want fighters to be able to recall good athletic bend and footwork under fatigued states; to that end, I ask fighters to show level changes and to move in and out with great coordination while fatigued. Second, shadow boxing serves as active recovery. Even though I am asking the fighters to move precisely, the fact that they are unloaded and can move freely with strikes and kicks helps facilitate the recovery of the waste by-products of lactate accumulation.

Table 12.11 Wednesday: Lactate and Muscular Endurance (Capacity and Power)

Training mode	Theme	Exercise selection	Sets and reps	Rest and recovery
Footwork and agility (one footwork drill and one agility drill)	Quick, precise effort; quality over quantity	Line hop, p. 169 Sprint ladder, p. 84 Pro shuttle, p. 21	Footwork: 2 × 5 reps (20 sec. per rep) Agility: 1 × 3 to 5	Footwork: Rest of 10 sec. between reps and 60 sec. between sets Agility: work-to-rest ratio of 1:3
Muscular endurance (lactate capacity) and total body for first three weeks of camp; deloading in week four	Submaximal effort but pushing the lactate threshold with total-body exercise paired in superset fashion	Superset 1 1a) Walking lunge, p. 134 1b) Bent-over row, p. 131 1c) Flat bench press, p. 100 1d) Three plank positions (prone), p. 90	2 or 3 × 12 to 20	1:1 work-to-rest ratio between sets or heart rate to 120 to 130 beats per min. Rest of 2 or 3 min. between supersets
		Superset 2 2a) Single-leg box blast, p. 140 2b) Suspension training inverted row, p. 114 2c) Push-up, p. 102 2d) Three plank positions (lateral), p. 90	2 or 3 × 12 to 20	
		Superset 3 3a) Shoulder press, p. 105 3b) Physioball partner push, p. 126 3c) Tall monster walk, p. 95	2 or 3 × 12 to 20	

(continued)

Table 12.12 *(continued)*

Training mode	Theme	Exercise selection	Sets and reps	Rest and recovery
Muscular endurance with speed and power emphasis; transition to lactate power in the last three weeks (weeks 5 to 7) to conclude camp; deloading in week 8 to taper to the fight	Submaximal to maximal effort in 30 to 90 sec. bursts of effort (one to three exercises at 30 sec. each)	Superset 1 1a) Sled push, p. 113 1b) Fat-grip horizontal row, p. 137 1c) Shadow boxing, p. 238 Superset 2 2a) 10 and 20 yd. (m) sprints, p. 20 2b) Heavy-bag carry, p. 136 2c) Shadow boxing, p. 238 Superset 3 3a) Landmine row to punch, p. 108 3b) Burpee, p. 146 3c) Towel curl to press, p. 98	30 sec. per exercise, total of 90 sec. of work with three pairings Repeated for 2 to 4 sets based on individual ability	Work-to-rest ratios: week 5—1:3; week 6—1:2; week 7—1:1 to 1.5 or heart rate to 120 to 130 beats per min.

Friday is our steady-state workout, but instead of road-running we stay in the same heart-rate zone but get much more productive work in the form of corrective, mobility, and stability exercise as you will see in table 12.12. This day is important because our fight team typically spars on Friday nights, but many teams save sparring for Saturday; therefore, I added this steady-state workout to serve as a pre-warm-up or opener before sparring. On fight night, we do an opener session to warm up the athlete so that the prefight warm-up is not the first time in the day that the fighter has prepared the body for physical work. In addition, in keeping with the SAID principle (specific adaptation to imposed demand), we have our sparring sessions mimic what we will be doing on the day of the fight.

Friday evening is when our MMA team tends to spar; as a result, the Friday training session serves as a warm-up for the sparring session later in the day. Most fighters do a workout on fight day (about five hours beforehand). Referred to as an opener, this is a light workout that mimics the structure of the fight-night warm-up, from general to specific. This approach helps combat fight-day nerves and, more important, sets the tone for the rest of the day, leading up to the fighter's arrival at the venue.

Table 12.12 Friday: Aerobic or Steady-State Mobility and Stability

Training mode	Theme	Exercise selection	Sets and reps	Rest and recovery
Footwork (one exercise used as a continuation of the warm-up)	Quick footwork and coordination	Medicine-ball toe touch, p. 170 Sprint ladder, p. 84 Box drill, p. 172	3 or 4 × 3 (30 sec., 20 sec., 10 sec.); increasing speed of reps as rep time decreases	2:1 work-to-rest ratio between reps 30 sec. rest between sets
Weights, bands, medicine balls	Low-intensity exercises paired in series of three to serve as active recovery, mobility, and stability training in preparation for end-of-week sparring (nice tempo without rushing)	Superset 1 1a) Zercher squat (light), p. 138 1b) Single-arm dumbbell row (moderate-heavy), p. 135 1c) Physioball roll-out, p. 93 Superset 2 2a) Bent-over T, p. 54 2b) Inchworm, p. 61 2c) Elbow to instep, p. 62 Superset 3 3a) Hip thrust, p. 110 3b) Elbow tap, p. 124 3c) Ankle rockers, p. 48	3 or 4 × 6 3 or 4 × 6 3 or 4 × 6	No rest for entire workout Heart rate between 130 and 150 beats per min. for entire workout
Recovery	Postsession self-myofascial release and active isolated range-of-motion stretching; barefoot cool-down	Foam roll, p. 186	Athlete autonomy to spend the necessary time	

The time between the Friday workout and the Friday evening sparring is exactly five hours. I specifically tell fighters that this workout is part of our injury prevention work but also serves as a warm-up before sparring—no fighter's t unlike the opener on fight night. This description helps set the mind-set going into the workout, as the fighter puts herself or himself in that place to which he or she must go on fight day.

PRE-FIGHT TAPER

Earlier in chapter 9, weekly undulating periodization or summated mesocycles were discussed. If you recall, it was 3-4 weeks of increased workload with a one week deload or a stair step approach. During the taper, however, I reverse the workload and ultimately create a step down approach of training volume to best prepare the athlete for a full recovery prior to the night of the fight.

There is a huge misconception that the last week prior to the fight is the taper. Most coaches throw the entire "kitchen sink" of workload at the fighter for seven weeks, and at the last week they back off on most work and expect the athlete to fully adapt to all the previous workloads. There are two key problems with this rationale:

1. One week is not enough time for full recovery for the intensive and extensive nature of training.

2. Most fighters are really starting to restrict calories about three weeks away from the fight, so now the nutritional recovery is less than optimal for how hard the training sessions are.

The key to an optimal taper is the complimentary reductions of training stress and the fine tuning of tactical and strategic application. Table 12.13 and table 12.14 will give the reader a sense of what the trend for the fight camp should look like from a training accumulation (12.13) and training reduction (12.14). The first block of training will resemble a three tier steady climb of workload, with the fourth week a deload. The start of week five is now a return of higher workload that mimics or is slightly greater than that of week three. Week six now starts the reduction of training volume, even though the taper is beginning here, the athletes won't recognize a change based on accumulative fatigue. Week seven is another reduction in cumulative workload and is when the athletes will really start to notice a significant change in volume. Week eight is the last week of workload, and now the total training volume is drastically reduced. However, the common theme from weeks 5-8 is the step down approach in workload but intensity (speed/load) remain high, this is of huge importance. If we take a look at training residuals, meaning the time for a performance quality to diminish, one of the first qualities that will diminish if stimulation is not adequate is speed. Earlier in this book, I mentioned that speed is the X factor in competition. Many coaches remove speed and strength qualities early in a taper and rely only on the tactical work for this quality to be retained. If done this way, the athlete could be going into battle with less ammunition at his or her disposal. Week nine is fight week! This means that the coach and athlete are finalizing the game plan and all training is only specific to the sport, but there is still a high demand for speed with tactical sessions.

The goal of the taper is to reduce workload, but preserve specific performance (speed/power) and technical qualities. Using the step down method is a great way to preserve the athletes ability while allowing them to optimally recover prior to the night of the fight.

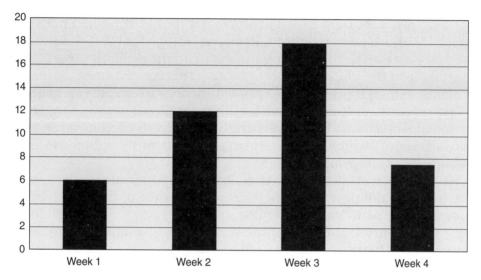

Figure 12.1   Showing a fight camp stair step up block of training (3:1)

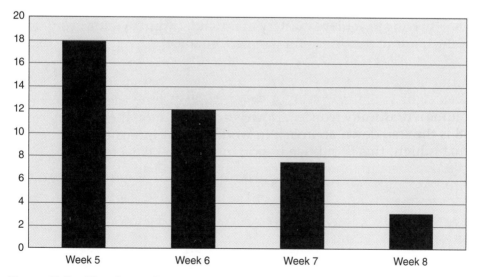

Figure 12.2   Showing stair step down block of training

CONCLUSION

The process of preparing an MMA athlete for a fight is both physical and mental. Everything you do should be done for a reason. Too many fighters feel that they must suffer in training camp in order to be the best prepared; this is simply not the case. Training camp preparation must produce a win-win outcome, meaning that work (both physical and mental) must be done, but that it is equally important to allow for recovery.

To simply work hard for eight weeks without a structured plan is a recipe for disaster when fight night arrives. I hope that this chapter has opened your eyes to the training variables and the thought process that must go into the journey to be your best. This is not a one-size-fits-all program; rather, it presents ideas and guidelines to enable you to build a best-practice approach in which athletes and coaches work together to prepare for a fight. The individual fighter's needs must be taken into consideration; avoid following a plan that some other fighter used just because he or she won a fight.

Finally, when evaluating the effectiveness of your training plan, wins and losses do not provide the best barometer. Some of the best training camps I have participated in ended up in a loss due to circumstances out of our control; similarly, some wins have come after a camp with the worst preparation. Analyze each training camp and note what went well and what could have gone better. Being realistic and constructively critical is the only way to evolve as a practitioner!

Thank you for joining me on this journey. This book offers my thoughts as I know them today. I will continue to evolve my vision while striving to achieve mastery in my craft by uncovering every stone in the quest to maximize human performance!

Index

About the Author

Loren Landow has been an athletic performance specialist for more than 20 years. He has trained over 500 professionals from the Ultimate Fighting Championship (UFC), National Football League, Major League Baseball, Major League Soccer, and National Hockey League, as well as Olympic gold medalists and a world-record holder.

Landow was the strength and conditioning coach on season 16 of *The Ultimate Fighter* reality television show. He is widely recognized as an authority on speed and power development and presents nationally and internationally for renowned organizations in the sport performance and fitness industries. He is often hired as a consultant for many club and professional teams. Currently, he is director of sport performance for the Steadman Hawkins Orthopedic Clinic in Denver, Colorado.

During his career, Landow has been fortunate to work with some of the best martial artists in the world, including UFC fighters Brendan Schaub, Neil Magny, Shane Carwin, Cat Zingano, Donald "Cowboy" Cerrone, Brandon Thatch, current bantamweight world champion T.J. Dillashaw, and Strikeforce champion Nate Marquardt. He has coached some of the top practitioners of Brazilian jiu-jitsu, muay tai, taekwondo, karate, judo, and Russian sambo along with world-class boxers and wrestlers.

Landow's philosophy is simple: Maximize human performance through efficiency. With a full arsenal of exercises and a leave-no-stone-unturned mentality, he aims for efficiency in training, which transfers to each athlete's specific sport or individual playing position. He firmly believes that speed, power, strength, agility, flexibility (mobility and stability), balance, and conditioning are biomotor skills an athlete must develop for success.